THE DEAD DON'T CRY

George J. Condon

gjcondon@checkmatefiction.com

http://www.checkmatefiction.com

Dedication:

To those living with depression
May you soon walk in the light

ONE

Something about the Raintree house made me think of Edgar Allan Poe. The building's dark mansards and gables had a brooding nineteenth century look that would've fit right into *The Fall Of The House Of Usher*. It didn't help that I saw the place outlined against a slate colored sky.

As I parked my midnight blue Toyota on the interlocking brick driveway, I felt uneasy in my gut. Maybe it was because I was in Rosedale, the kind of rich Toronto neighborhood where peasants like me get arrested for loitering. Maybe it was because I was still having bad dreams about my last case. Whatever the reason, I told myself to get a grip. This was just another job.

I turned up my tweed overcoat's collar against the wind, locked the Toyota and walked up to the front door. It was three o'clock on a November afternoon and the air was less frosty than that morning. Snow was probably on the way. I pushed the gold colored doorbell button and waited while gusts of wind made withered leaves skitter and dance across the huge front lawn.

The door was opened by a slim gray haired woman wearing a navy blue blazer over her white blouse and banker's gray skirt. If forced to guess, I would have placed her somewhere in her early seventies. Her posture and expression signalled that she was accustomed to being treated with deference.

"Yes?" she asked.

"Mrs. Raintree?"

"That's who I am. Who are you?"

"Matthew Ryan."

I held out one of my business cards and Rebecca Raintree shoved it into a pocket of her jacket without looking at it.

"You're punctual, Mr. Ryan. I like that. Please come in."

We walked down a blue carpeted hallway, then turned left into a large room filled with overstuffed floral pattern furniture. Tiffany lamps sat on a couple of oak end tables, while old black and white photographs stood in a row on the dark marble mantle above the hearth. Two oil paintings of hunting scenes hung on one wall. In one corner, a pendulum clock ticked. Time had stopped here more than fifty years ago.

Mrs. Raintree pointed to an easychair.

"Please have a seat, Mr. Ryan."

As I pulled my overcoat off and sat down, she lowered herself carefully into a chair that faced mine. Her slow, stiff movements made me suspect severe arthritis. She looked at me solemnly.

"I'd offer you some coffee, but I gave my Beatrice the day off. She does everything for me in the kitchen."

I put on what I hoped was my most charming expression.

"That's all right. I'm not much of a coffee drinker."

Mrs. Raintree folded her hands in her lap. She seemed to be unsure of what to say next.

"Are you a good detective, Mr. Ryan?"

"I try to be."

"You haven't really answered my question."

"I think I'm a very good detective, but I'm biased."

The old lady nodded, apparently satisfied.

"Naturally, I'll expect you to be very discreet."

"Why don't you tell me what you want me to do, Mrs. Raintree? Then we can talk about discretion."

For just a moment, the woman's mask of imperiousness slipped, letting her pain and weariness show through.

"I want you to find my son."

From an inside blazer pocket, she pulled out a passport size photo and handed it to me. I saw the image of a worried looking man who had dark hair that was receding from his forehead.

"How long has he been missing?" I asked.

"A week. He went to work last Thursday and never came home."

"Have you contacted the police?"

"Of course. I don't think they're trying hard enough to find David."

"How old is your son?"

"Thirty-six."

"Where does he live?"

"Here, with me."

"Has he been in any trouble lately?"

"Of course not. David's a good boy."

"Is it possible he just went away on a holiday?"

"David would never go anywhere without telling me."

"What does David do for a living?"

"He's a corporate lawyer."

"Has he seemed worried or upset lately?"

"No more than usual. David is very sensitive."

"Is there something you're not telling me, Mrs. Raintree?"

The old lady's face took on that weary look again.

"Over the years, David has had problems with drugs and alcohol. Things got worse after Howard ... after my husband died, but David has put all that behind him now. He's been in a recovery program for two years now."

I began to understand why the police weren't putting too much effort into finding a thirty-six year old mamma's boy who used drugs and alcohol. The cops probably thought David was shooting it up or getting drunk in some cheap motel. They were probably right.

"I wasn't too worried at first, Mr. Ryan. Then I found the message."

"Message?"

"Yes. You must understand that I never touch any of David's things ordinarily. I looked around in his room this time because I hoped to discover something that would tell me where he was. I found this in with some other papers on his desk."

She handed me a folded piece of printer paper. I opened it and saw nine words in capitals: *WE HAVE TO PAY FOR WHAT WE HAVE DONE.*

"What does it mean, Mr. Ryan?"

"I'm sorry, Mrs. Raintree, but I've no idea."

"Will you find my son for me?"

I looked at Rebecca Raintree and tried to think of the nicest way to let her down. Experience told me to avoid David's sorry life and to get out of his mother's house as soon as possible. This kind of case wouldn't be all that interesting and was sure to end badly for the client.

"I'll pay you double your regular fee, Mr. Ryan. Plus all of your expenses, of course."

I thought about how much money that was and remembered the state of my agency's bank account.

"I'll get right on it," I said.

TWO

Mickey Finn's is an ersatz Irish pub in the Village By The Grange, a neighborhood on the outskirts of Chinatown. The pub is close to Toronto Police Service 52 Division, so a lot of Metro cops drop in there for a few beers after they come off duty. I suspect some of them drop in for a few beers while they're still on duty, but that's not my business.

It was lunch hour and Mickey's had a corned beef special, so I was lucky to get a table, even one positioned near the door to the toilets. The dark wooden bar looks authentic enough and I'm told that the house serves a good draft beer, though I've never tried it. Unfortunately, somebody decided Mickey's would seem more Irish with pictures of leprechauns and shamrocks festooning the walls. As I looked around, I found myself wishing my family had come from Budapest instead of Dublin.

I recognized a few of the men from 52 Division at other tables, but they ignored me. I'm not on the best of terms with the force these days. I'll spare you the details. Being ignored by the boys in blue was fine with me because I wasn't at Mickey's to socialize with them. I was waiting for Detective Sergeant Joe Beck.

The street door opened and Beck lumbered in wearing a navy pea jacket over a gray fisherman's knit sweater and brown pants. Even in civilian clothes, he advertised himself as a cop by wearing his regulation issue shoes. Beck was a bear of a man who must have played football in high school. Though he was still powerfully built, years of riding around in squad cars had shifted a lot of his bulk to his gut and rump.

Usually, Beck had no time for civilians, especially private investigators like me. He made an exception in my case because I'd helped him out once when he was being questioned by the Special Investigations Unit about an accusation he'd beaten a suspect he'd collared. I've got no sympathy for brutal cops, but I was parked nearby on a stakeout and saw the whole thing go down.

I saw the perp throw the first punch, before Beck decked him in self defense. I came forward to testify on the big cop's behalf. If Beck had been in the wrong, I like to think I would have testified anyway.

Beck stood in the doorway for a minute while his eyes adjusted to the dimmer light inside Mickey's. When he saw me, he walked over to my table.

"Hello, Ryan. I see you're still alive. The hoods in this town must be getting sloppy."

"You're still the same old charmer, Beck. Pull up a chair."

Beck sat down and I waved at one of the waiters. He was a thin college kid who wore his hair in a pony tail and sported a nose ring. The kid came over to our table and stood there, waiting for our orders.

"Kilkenny Draft," Beck said. "Not too cold."

"Sure." The kid turned to look at me.

"San Pelligrino with a twist of lime."

The waiter nodded and headed for the bar. Beck looked at me and grunted.

"Mineral water? That's a fairy's drink, Ryan."

"I decided it was time to come out of the closet."

"Now that I think of it, I've never seen you drink booze. Got religion or something?"

I decided not to tell Beck about my years as an alcoholic or the depression medication I was taking. Some things I'll admit only to people I trust. Beck hadn't quite made it into that select group yet.

"Alcohol doesn't agree with me," I said.

"No shit? So, why am I here?"

"Can't I ask you to have a drink without having an agenda?"

"Maybe, if you weren't a tricky gumshoe who has more twists in him than a corkscrew. What do you want?"

"All right. I've been hired by a Mrs. Raintree to find her missing son David. Know anything about the case?"

"It's not one of mine, but I know about it. We have two good men working it, Ryan. Just leave things to the police."

"Mrs. Raintree doesn't think the police are giving the case enough priority. That's why she hired me."

"Know how many missing persons cases we have open?"

"I'm not saying she's right, Beck. Still, she can hire me if she likes."

"She can piss up a rope if she likes. You want me to find Raintree for you, is that it?"

The waiter interrupted while he put our drinks down onto the table. His pockmarked face split into a grin when I handed him fifteen bucks and told him to keep the change. He scooted away before I could change my mind.

"I just want to know what your guys have found out so far," I told Beck. "I don't want to go over old ground and get in your way."

"You always get in our way, Ryan."

Beck took a swallow of his beer, then coughed and made a face.

"Jesus Christ! I told that punk waiter I didn't want my beer too cold. This is a Popsicle."

He leaned forward and lowered his voice.

"No hard feelings, Buddy, but this case isn't worth your time. Old Lady Raintree's son is a dope head and a drunk. Guys like him disappear all the time when they go on benders. Right now, David Raintree is lying in some doorway, guzzling a bottle of Old Sailor."

"Maybe, but there was this message in his papers."

I handed Beck a copy of the note Mrs. Raintree had given to me. Beck glanced at it, then tossed it back.

"Who knows what it means, if it means anything at all?"

"Can't you give me anything at all, Beck?"

"All right. I guess I owe you. Maybe we aren't looking too hard for Raintree, but we are looking. We've questioned his friends. It's not a long list of names."

"Like who?"

"Two guys named Weisman and Holt went to a pansy prep school with Raintree, about twenty years ago. A place called The Shawncrest Academy For Boys. Even the name makes me want to puke. Weisman and Holt stayed in touch with Raintree, but they're not all as tight as they used to be. Holt was out of town when we went looking for him, but we questioned Weisman. You might want to talk to the guy. I think he knows more than he was saying."

"Where can I find him?"

"Call Constable Eddie Howard on the desk at 52 Division. Tell him Beck said to give you Weisman's address and telephone number. That's the best I can do for you."

"Thanks. I hope Santa will be good to you this Christmas."

Beck took another swig of beer, then he grinned at me.

"I ran a background check on you, Ryan."

"On me? Why?"

"I like to know who I'm dealing with. There's always been something a little mysterious about you. That bothers me."

"I don't know what you mean, Beck. I'm an open book."

"Really? I found out you did time in the military."

"That's no big secret. If you'd asked, I'd have told you."

"Maybe, but when I tried to find out what you did in the service, I was told the Ministry Of Defense sealed your file."

"Well, you know how secretive bureaucrats can be."

"When the military seals somebody's file, it means one of two things. Either the guy was doing something top secret or he got himself into some really deep shit. Which was it with you, Ryan?"

"Exactly," I said.

THREE

It was around two o'clock in the afternoon when I drove back to my office. As I went north on Yonge Street, pale winter sunshine was surrendering to dark clouds scudding in from the west. A few large snowflakes drifted down, but the weather station on my car's radio didn't predict any serious accumulation.

Christmas was less than five weeks away and the stores along Yonge Street were decked out in lights and tinsel already. Window signs touted sales that would save me huge amounts of money if I bought loads of merchandise that I didn't need or want. Capitalism has always understood the real meaning of Christmas.

I work out of a low rise business mall just off Gordon Baker Road. Midway down the main hall, you'll find a door with frosted glass panels and *Ryan Investigations* spelled out in black letters. The good thing about the location is that rents are much lower than they are downtown. The bad thing is that North York is about as familiar to most of my clients as the dark side of the Moon.

Samantha was working at her computer when I walked in. She looked alluring in her powder blue turtle neck and a snug black skirt that was slit up one side. With her face and figure, Samantha would look alluring in a potato sack. When she saw me, she pushed an unruly lock of red hair back from her forehead and smiled.

"Hello, Sherlock."

I didn't pay her enough for a respectful greeting.

"Hi, Sam. Any calls while I was out?"

"Two. Mr. Crombie says there'll be trouble if you don't send his investigation report by the end of the week. Somebody named Felicia called from Trafalgar Realty. She says our rent check bounced again and they may take legal action."

"Sounds pretty routine. I'll deal with both of them after I read the mail."

"Matt, I'll be in late tomorrow. I've got to take Theresa to an orthodontist. She needs braces on her teeth."

I noticed that Samantha was telling me, not asking me. We both knew I'd be helpless around the office without her, so I didn't pretend to have a choice. Besides, being a single mother couldn't be easy for Samantha.

"Okay, Sam. Don't be surprised if Theresa acts a little moody afterwards. Wearing braces is tough for a nine year old."

"I know. I wore them when I was a little girl and just hated them. Thanks for being so thoughtful, Matt."

Samantha gave me a smile that made my knees weak, then she went back to her computer work. I wished she didn't get to me so easily.

The mail wasn't interesting, just the usual bills and a few advertising fliers. One letter told me I might have won a publisher's sweepstakes. Call me a skeptic, but I doubted that very much.

As Sergeant Beck had suggested, I called Eddie Howard at 52 Division and got Eric Weisman's address and phone number. When I rang the number Eddie gave to me, nobody answered. I changed my mind about spending my afternoon in the office and decided I'd go over to Weisman's place to try to catch him in.

According to Eddie, Weisman made and sold jewelry for a living. He lived in rooms above his small shop near the intersection of Bloor and Bathurst. As I drove out there, the day had darkened into the gray winter twilight so typical of winter in Toronto. It's the kind of washed out light that makes the world look bleak and hopeless. Even the gaudy neon signs along the city streets couldn't overcome the gloom.

I found a parking spot across the street from a store with the sign "Weisman Jewelry Limited" out front. After locking my Toyota, I fed some coins into the nearest parking meter before I walked to the corner to cross the street with the traffic light. I was in a very law abiding mood.

There was a *CLOSED* sign in the shop's window, but the front door opened when I pushed on it. Except for melodic door chimes, I heard no sound as I walked in. Inside, the air was dry and musty. The lights were on and pieces of jewelry glittered in glass cases, but nobody came out to greet me. I called out Weisman's name a couple of times, but got no answer. At the back of the store, I saw a flight of stairs leading to an upper floor.

The old wooden stairs had a worn carpet covering and they creaked under my weight as I climbed them. When I reached the landing, I saw an open doorway on my right and walked through it into a small, shabbily furnished room. As soon as I entered the room, I saw Weisman. He sat on a dilapidated gray couch and it smelled as though he'd been sitting there for at least three or four days. Once you've been exposed to the sticky sweet stench of putrefying human flesh, the memory of it never leaves you.

A pump action shotgun lay on the carpet. Somebody had used at least one load from it on Weisman. I won't describe what buckshot does to a man's face from close range. If you ever see that, you won't think about eating again for at least a couple of days.

As I fought the urge to vomit, I noticed no sign of a struggle in the room. For a moment, I thought Weisman might have killed himself, then I saw something that destroyed that notion.

Someone had dipped his finger into the splatter of blood and brains on the wall behind Weisman's body to trace out the word <u>hangman</u> in a large red scrawl.

The sight and smell of Weisman's corpse were too much. I stumbled back downstairs with the taste of bile in my mouth. After I'd fished my cellphone out of my overcoat, I called 911. There was nothing for me to do then but wait for the police.

FOUR

Downstairs in the shop, I sat on a brown wooden chair I'd found behind of one of the jewellry display cases. From there, I could look outside through the shop's plate glass window, so I noticed the patrol car as soon as it pulled up at the curb. Two stocky cops wearing bullet proof vests got out. One of them was blond, while his partner was dark haired. Both of them seemed to be painfully young, but everyone is beginning to look that way to me. The cops entered the jewellry shop slowly with their service pistols drawn, not taking chances. I was careful not to make any quick moves.

"You the one who called this in?" the blond cop asked me.

"That's right. The body's upstairs. First door on the right."

Blondie nodded to his dark haired partner who went upstairs to check out my story. Relaxing a little, the blond cop put away his gun and took out a thick black notebook.

"Want to tell me what happened here, Buddy?"

"Sure. The front door was unlocked. I came in and found the body. That's about it."

"No kidding? Who are you and what were you doing here?"

I pulled out one of my business cards and handed it to the cop.

"I'm a private detective. I wanted to talk to Weisman about one of my cases. Somebody else got to him first."

Just then, Blondie's partner came back downstairs, looking a little green around the gills.

"Jesus, Stan! It's ugly up there," he said. "I called the coroner's office. They're sending a meat wagon with a medical examiner. What's this guy's story?"

I went through my whole song and dance again for the dark haired cop. When I finished, he nodded to his partner.

"I don't think he's the shooter, Stan, unless he's been here before. That stiff has been there for at least a few days "

About ten minutes later, an Emergency Medical Services ambulance stopped out front, followed by a black sedan. Two male paramedics in dark blue uniforms and a woman wearing white coveralls climbed out of the ambulance, while Sergeant Beck got out of the sedan. He nodded when he saw me.

"Are you working Homicide these days, Beck?" I asked.

"No, but I came over anyway when I heard you were involved."

"Whatever Weisman knew, he can't tell me now," I said.

"You need to control yourself, Ryan. I expected you to just question the guy, not blow his fucking head off."

"Very funny. Were there people who wanted to kill Weisman?"

"Obviously, there was at least one. We didn't run much of a check on Weisman. He was just somebody we questioned about the Raintree case. You'd never know it by looking at this dump, but he came from a ritzy family. His father was a hotshot surgeon over at Mount Sinai Hospital."

"You told me Weisman went to school with David Raintree."

"Yeah. Like I said, a snobby prep school near Ottawa. The Shawncrest Academy For Boys. That was about twenty years ago."

"Are Weisman's parents still alive?" I asked.

"No. There's just a sister named Laura. She's a doctor and she lives in one of them luxury penthouse complexes downtown. Somebody will have to tell her about her brother."

Just then, the woman in white coveralls came back downstairs, wearing bloodstained latex gloves on her hands. Beck called to her and she walked over to us. She was somewhere in her late forties, slim with black hair that was streaked by gray. Her face had the tired, haunted look of somebody who sees too many people lying in pools of their own blood.

"Ryan, this is Dr. Ellen Paladini," Beck said. "What have you found out, Doc?"

"The victim died about four days ago. I can't pin down the exact time of death after this long. The cause of death was a gunshot wound to the head."

"Anything else?"

"The shotgun likely belongs to the victim. We found a box of shells and a cleaning rag near the couch where he died."

"You mean the guy was stupid enough to clean a loaded shotgun?"

"People do it more often than you'd think, Sergeant Beck. That's not what I think happened this time."

"So, what did happen?"

"Let me try to guess," I said. "Weisman was home alone, cleaning his shotgun. It was probably late at night. That's why the sign in the window says the shop is closed. Weisman heard somebody knock at the shop door and he came downstairs. His visitor was somebody he knew, so Weisman let him come in. That's why there are no signs of forced entry."

"And he had a fight with the shooter?" Beck asked.

"I doubt it. There are no signs of a stuggle. I think the killer went upstairs with Weisman on some pretext. Weisman left the room and his killer noticed the shotgun. It was too good an opportunity to pass up. The killer loaded the gun, then put it back down beside the couch. When Weisman came back, the killer let him sit down, then he picked up the shotgun and blew Weisman away."

"It could have gone down like that," Dr. Paladini said.

"Doctor, did you notice the word 'hangman' scrawled on the wall in blood?" I asked.

"Yes. Obviously, Weisman didn't write that. The killer might have done it. What does it mean?"

"I don't know, but I intend to find out."

"Play Sherlock Holmes all you like," Beck said. "Just don't hinder our investigation."

"I wouldn't dream of it. Do you need me for anything else?"

"You can go for now, Ryan. Stay in touch."

"Will Constable Howard know where I can find Weisman's sister?"

"Sure, but wait until after we talk to her first."

"No problem. So long, Beck. Nice meeting you, Dr. Paladini."

"And you, Mr. Ryan."

I walked outside and crossed the street to where I'd parked my car. Though it was only about five o'clock, it was dark already. The short daylight hours are the worst of northern winters. For a moment, I sat silently behind the steering wheel, still shaken by the horror in Weisman's shop. Finally, I started up my Toyota, switched on its headlights and pulled away from the curb.

FIVE

Despite the evening rush hour, I made it back to my office in fairly good time. It was a cloudy night with overcast skies that blocked out any stars. The office lights were still on and Samantha was shutting down her computer when I walked in. Through the open doorway to our conference room, I saw a little girl whose red hair was styled in braids. She looked like Samantha in miniature as she sat at the oval table we use for client meetings and played with a handheld video game. Samantha looked embarrassed.

"I'm sorry about bringing Tess here, Matt. By the time we finished at the orthodontist, her school was closed."

"Don't worry about it, Sam."

I walked to the door of the conference room and stepped inside.

"You must be Theresa," I said, smiling at the little girl.

She looked up from her game.

"My friends call me 'Tess'"

"My name's Matt. May I call you 'Tess'?"

She thought about that for a moment, then shrugged.

"I guess that would be all right."

"I hear that you got braces today, Tess."

It was the wrong thing to say. Theresa looked down at her hands and I thought she was going to cry.

"Yes. The doctor says I have to wear them all the time."

"I guess other girls at school will envy you."

Theresa looked at me as though I was an idiot.

"Why will they do that?"

"Because all the Hollywood actresses wore braces when they were little."

"They did?"

"Sure. Why do you think they all have such beautiful, straight teeth now?"

Theresa looked at me as though wondering whether I was teasing her. Finally, she smiled, displaying her new braces.

"I didn't know that," she said.

"Well, you do now."

I heard movement behind me and turned to see Samantha standing in the doorway.

"We have to go now, Tess. Say goodbye to Mr. Ryan."

Theresa switched off her video game and put it into a pocket of her coat. She looked up at me and smiled again.

"Goodbye, Mr. Ryan."

"Please call me Matt."

"All right. Goodbye, Matt."

Theresa walked out of the room. Samantha started after her, then she turned back to face me.

"I overheard what you told Tess. Thank you."

"Don't mention it."

"Would you have dinner with us on Sunday?"

I was caught by surprise and answered without thinking.

"Sure."

"Wonderful. We can discuss the details later. Good night, Matt."

After Theresa and Samantha left, I sat at my desk and thought about the Raintree case. Maybe I'd been wrong to assume that David Raintree was missing only because he'd gone back to using drugs. The person who killed Weisman might be responsible for Raintree's disappearance too. If I wanted to keep David alive, I had to find him fast. Trolling through his phone records or looking for any activity on his credit card might take too long, though I planned to have Samantha do those things anyway.

As I closed up the office, I wanted to kick myself for not finding an excuse to refuse Samantha's dinner invitation. Socializing with Samantha was something I scrupulously avoided. She was just so damned attractive that I didn't trust myself not to do something to embarrass both of us. I didn't need more grief in my life. Sometime before Sunday, I'd have to invent a reason for not being able to go to her house.

SIX

The law offices of *Pierce, Taylor And Berenger* are on the fifteenth floor of one of the Toronto-Dominion Center's towers. As I rode upwards in the elevator, a computer generated voice announced each floor. The voice sounded so calm and confident that I was about to ask for financial advice when the elevator door opened.

I turned left into a wide corridor and waded through ankle deep royal blue carpet until I reached the reception area. A chubby young Asian woman who sat behind a mahogany desk looked up and smiled at me. Her smile seemed genuine, but I'm putty in the hands of women, so I wouldn't know for sure.

"Good afternoon, Sir. May I help you?"

I handed one of my business cards to her.

"I have an appointment to see Mr. Berenger at two."

"Of course, Mr. Ryan. Let me make sure that he's in."

She picked up her telephone and pressed a red button.

"Mr. Berenger? There's a Mr. Ryan here to see you. Yes, I'll send him right in."

She put down her phone and gave me another smile.

"Mr. Berenger will see you now. Just go through those glass doors, turn right, then walk to the end of the corridor."

"Thank you, Gwen."

For a second, Gwen looked startled that I knew her name, then she must have remembered the brass identity plate on her desk.

"I guess you're a good detective, Mr. Ryan."

"Sherlock Holmes is envious."

Geoffrey Berenger had the kind of big corner office you'd expect for a senior law partner. Very likely, he had a spectacular view of the city on a clear day. When I walked in, everything more than a meter or two outside the windows was being obscured by a snow squawl.

Berenger sat behind a desk that seemed the size of an aircraft carrier's flight deck. He looked the very model of a successful corporate lawyer with his gray hair, expensive dark blue suit and prep school necktie. There must be a factory somewhere that churns out corporate weasels. With a few minor variations, they all seem the same to me, right down to the phoney smile and vise grip handshake.

Berenger rose to give me the regulation handshake, then he sat down again. Leaning back in his swivel chair, he rested his shiny black leather Guccis on his desk.

"Please have a seat, Mr. Ryan."

He waved at an office chair near his desk. I sat down, aware that the chair had probably cost more than I earn in a month.

"I'm new at this," Berenger said. "I'm not used to dealing with ... What do you people call yourselves? 'Private dicks'?"

"The term 'investigator' will do fine."

"Of course. How can I help you?"

"I'm sure you know David Raintree is missing. His mother hired me to find him. David works for your firm, so I hoped you might know what would make him decide to disappear. Was he in any trouble at the office?"

"I'm sorry, Mr. Ryan, but I don't know David that well. It's true he has worked here at PT&B for ten years, but he's not a full partner. He reports to Harvey Taylor. Harvey's on vacation in the Bahamas, so he couldn't meet with you. He asked me to fill in for him."

"I appreciate your doing that."

Berenger picked up a gold pen and tapped it absently against the top of his desk.

"To be brutally honest, Mr. Ryan, Harvey is thinking of letting David go. The quality of David's work has slipped badly during the last few months. The firm supported David when he had problems with alcohol and drugs, but we're not a charity. We have a right to expect a minimum standard of performance from our staff."

"Naturally. Is there anyone here who <u>has</u> worked closely with David?"

"You might want to speak to Walter Chong. He's helped David with some contracts. Walter's cubicle is back toward the reception area. Turn left at the water cooler."

"Thank you, Mr. Berenger," I said as I stood up. "I won't take up any more of your time."

"Glad to be of help."

He hadn't been much help at all. When I reached the door of his office, he put down his pen and cleared his throat.

"Tell me something, Mr. Ryan. Is being a detective really the way it's shown on TV? Dealing with dangerous criminals and sexy blonds all the time."

"Yes, but there are some exciting days too," I said and left the room.

When I found Walter Chong's cubicle, he was talking on the telephone, so I took a seat and waited. Chong was a slim Chinese man who appeared to be in his late twenties. His shoe brush haircut and one gold earring clashed with his conservative gray suit and sky blue tie. After he hung up the phone, I handed him one of my business cards.

"Geoff Berenger told me you've worked with David Raintree."

Chong shrugged.

"You could say that. Working with that dude is always a little weird. He isn't too tightly wrapped, if you know what I mean."

"Can you think of any reason why he'd want to disappear?"

"No, but I did freak him out about two weeks ago."

"What happened?"

"I was on lunch break, reading *The Globe And Mail*. I saw a story about David's old prep school, a place with some arty farty name."

"The Shawncrest Academy For Boys?"

"Yeah, that's it. The newspaper article said the school's administration was planning some renovations to the grounds. I showed the story to David because I thought he might be interested. Well, he went white as a freakin' ghost. After that, he was jumpy and distracted all the time."

"Any idea why he'd react like that?"

"Search me. The guy is a little off kilter at the best of times. Maybe you should talk to his girlfriend."

"I didn't know he had one."

"Well, he comes into the office now and again with some babe. I just assumed they were a number. She's a little old for me. Early thirties. Still, she's a real hottie. I've thought about asking her for a date. No idea what she sees in David."

"Do you know her name?"

"Laura something."

"Laura Weisman?"

"Yeah, I think that's it."

"Thanks, Walter. You've been a big help."

"You think something happened to David, Mr. Ryan?"

"I hope not, but it's starting to look that way."

Walter licked his lips, then asked what I knew he would.

"What's it like being a private detective?"

"Talk to Mr. Berenger. He can fill you in."

I left Walter looking puzzled, found the elevator and rode back down to the building's lobby. Cold air hit me like an electric shock as I stepped outside. I pulled my overcoat on and started toward the nearest subway station. For the moment, the snow had stopped and there was just a thin white carpet on the city pavement.

Ahead of me, two beefy men were unloading boxes from a black delivery van parked at the curb. Both wore black wool watch caps and dark blue parkas. Neither of them seemed to have shaved within the past three days. As I walked by, the taller man tossed his box into the back of the van and pulled a pack of cigarettes from a pocket of his parka. He shoved a cigarette between his lips and walked toward me.

"Hey, *Tovarishch*," he said in a heavy accent. "You got a light?"

I noticed his partner moving toward me too and I smelled a trap, but it was too late. The man with the cigarette hit me in the belly and I doubled over. As I struggled to breathe, I felt something ice cold pressed against the side of my head. The second man had pulled out a black pistol.

"Do what you are told," the gunman said. "Else you lose your brains."

The two goons pulled my arms behind my back, manacled my wrists together with handcuffs, then threw me into the back of their van. I landed face down on the metal floor as I heard the vehicle's rear clamshell doors slam shut behind me. A moment later, we lurched into motion as the van sped away from the curb.

SEVEN

I was inside the black van for what seemed like hours, but was probably about thirty minutes. The interior of the cargo area was robin's egg blue and streaks of rust showed in places where the paint had been scraped away. There were still a few of the big cardboard boxes on board and they tumbled around whenever the vehicle leaned into a turn in the road. One of the boxes fell onto me, but it was empty. Those containers had been just props in a little charade the two thugs had played until I was close enough to grab. By bracing my feet against one of the van's walls, I managed to prop myself into a sitting position. It wasn't very comfortable, but better than being flat on my belly.

Whenever the driver stopped for a traffic light, I thought about escape. Aside from the challenge of unlatching the back doors with my hands manacled behind my back, I didn't relish the idea of rolling out into the traffic on a busy street. I decided to stay where I was. My main worry was about what my captors would do when we reached our destination. Whatever they had planned for me, I didn't expect to enjoy it.

Finally, we stopped and the driver turned off the van's engine. A moment later, the rear doors opened and I turned my head to see the

two unshaven men peering in at me. The shorter one grinned, showing off a few gold teeth.

"Get out, *Tovarishch*. Be quick or we drag you."

I slid myself across the metal floor to the doorway, where the men pulled me out and lifted me into a standing position. They frog marched me up a wide driveway to the front door of a sprawling brick mansion. The house had a row of Grecian columns across its front that wouldn't have looked out of place in the movie <u>Gone</u> <u>With</u> <u>The</u> <u>Wind</u>.

When we reached the front door, the taller thug pressed the doorbell button and we waited. A moment later, the door was opened by a giant who wore his blond hair in a crew cut. He had a wrestler's beefy body and his face seemed to have been hacked from a block of granite. The shorter goon spoke to Stone Face in what I guessed was Russian and the huge man gestured for me to step inside. He growled something to my captors and they removed my handcuffs.

When my kidnappers tried to follow me into the house, Stone Face spoke to them in a way that sounded threatening and the pair hurried back to their vehicle. The minions had brought me, as ordered. Now, they were being dismissed. After he closed the front door behind us, Stone Face wrapped his huge right hand around my left arm. He had a grip like a garbage compactor as he pulled me down a long corridor and through a wide doorway into a large, carpeted room.

On my left, the wall was lined by dark wooden shelves filled with expensively bound books. On my right, I saw an enormous home theater screen. It was the wall directly in front of me that caught my attention. The most colorful butterfly collection I'd ever seen was mounted there, inside of three backlit glass cases.

In the center of the room, two chocolate colored easy chairs had been placed inside a cream colored circle woven into the burgundy carpet. A stocky gray haired man wearing blue silk pajamas sat in one of the chairs. He held a white china cup in his right hand while he read a magazine. Seeing me, the man smiled, then put his cup and magazine down on a teak table nearby.

"Hello, Mr. Ryan. Please sit down. It is good of you to come."

"I had some encouragement," I said as I sat in the other chair.

"I hope my men were not rough with you."

"Not at all. After they punched me in the gut, jammed a gun to my head and threw me into the back of their van, they were like perfect gentlemen."

The gray haired man frowned.

"Such treatment was unnecessary. Ivan and Victor are sometimes useful to me, but they are stupid men. They were told to use force only if you resisted. Would you like some coffee?"

"Thanks, but I'd rather know why I'm here."

"Right to business, eh? I like that. Do you know who I am?"

"I've seen your picture in the papers. You're Yuri Kursov."

"So, I am famous. Do you know what I do for living?"

"You're a loan shark."

"Please. That is ugly name. I am business man who helps those who need money. Is it so terrible?"

"That depends on what happens when they can't pay you back."

Kursov looked at me with eyes as cold as ice.

"One way or other, they always pay, Mr. Ryan."

"I don't doubt it."

Kursov picked up his coffee cup.

"How were you involved with Eric Weisman?"

"I wasn't."

"It is stupid to lie. My men are good at squeezing truth out of liars. You do not want to learn their methods."

"I'm not lying. I never met Weisman."

"You were at his place when you found his body."

"True, but I was interested in him only because he went to school with someone."

I gave Kursov a brief summary of the Raintree case to date. It didn't take long. So far, there wasn't much to tell. When I was finished, the gray haired gangster took a sip of coffee and looked at me for a moment.

"Interesting. Either you are very good liar or you tell truth, Mr. Ryan. For now, I will believe the second thing."

"Now you know my interest in Weisman, Kursov. What's yours?"

"That is not your business. Still, I will tell you. Eric liked to gamble, but he was not very good at it. He lost many times."

"And you were there to lend him money. Very noble of you. How much was he into you for?"

"One hundred thousand dollars."

"That's a lot of cash. More than enough to make you blow his face off with a shotgun."

"You insult me, Mr. Ryan. It would be stupid for me to kill Weisman. Dead men cannot pay me."

"What if Weisman wasn't going to pay anyway?"

"Then I would change his mind. Maybe cut off a finger, but not kill him."

"Either you are very good liar or you tell truth, Mr. Kursov. For now, I will believe the second thing."

"Do you make fun of me? You are a funny man, Mr. Ryan. Sometimes things happen to funny men to make them stop laughing."

"I'll remember that. May I go now?"

Kursov waved his hand in a dismissive gesture.

"Of course."

"That's quite a butterfly collection that you have," I said as I stood up to leave.

Kursov looked as though I'd paid him a great compliment.

"Are they not beautiful? I collect them for fifteen years now. Do you know anything about butterflies?"

"Not a thing."

"When they are grown, they eat nothing. A few sips of plant nectar maybe. When they are still caterpillars, they eat all the time. I have a country place where I breed my pets. When people annoy me, I take them there to feed them to the caterpillars."

Maybe Kursov was joking, but his butterfly collection lost its luster for me all the same. I started to leave the room. Stone Face had been waiting by the door and he moved to block me, but Kursov said something to him in Russian and the giant relaxed. I turned back to face Kursov.

"If you ever want to see me again, don't send your goons. A phone call will be enough."

"That may depend on why I want you, Mr. Ryan. Good night."

I walked out onto the front steps of the house, buttoning up my overcoat against the chill air. Despite my tough guy act inside, I had been very scared. I shivered now as the tension ebbed slowly from my body. I knew that Kursov had ties to the Russian Mafia, a group that makes Hell's Angels look like choir boys. Walking out of his house alive and with all of my body parts meant I was getting off very lightly. Next time, I might not be so lucky.

I didn't buy Kursov's story completely. Maybe Weisman had owed the Russian gangster a lot of money, but that situation became null and void when Weisman died. Kursov was after something else, but I didn't know what it was. Unless it involved the Raintree case, I didn't care.

Asking Kursov's thugs for a lift home didn't seem like a good idea, so I pulled my cellphone out of my overcoat and called for a taxi.

EIGHT

As the blue and cream taxi wound its way through city traffic, my paunchy driver complained about the roads, the weather and the government. He was a talkative Pakistani who told me he'd been an engineer in his native country. Here, he had to drive a taxi for a living. Unfortunately, it's a common story. The driver seemed delighted to have found a captive audience. I was relieved when we reached the parking lot where I'd left my Toyota.

"And that's why an honest man like me cannot make a decent living here," the driver said as he stopped his cab at the curb.

"It's a dirty shame."

I reached into my coat and pulled out my billfold. After I gave my driver his fare, plus the obligatory tip, I left his cab.

"Have a nice Christmas," the driver said before he drove away.

"Not for four more weeks," I called after him.

After I got into my car, I decided to use my cellphone to call my office and check for voice mail. Samantha surprised me by picking up after the first ring.

"Ryan Investigations."

"Hello, Sam. Any calls?"

"Where have you been, Matt? I've been trying to reach you all morning."

"It's a long story. What's happening?"

"That Felicia person called again from Trafalgar Realty. She's a real bitch. This time, it seems they're really serious about legal action over the rent."

I remembered the bank deposit I'd made from Mrs. Raintree's cash advance. For a change, we had some money in our company account.

"All right, Sam. Cut them a check. We should be good for it. Oh, and that report Crombie's been chasing us about is on my desk. Just give it a quick proof read, then send it out. Thanks."

"Matt, I have something about the Raintree case."

"Great. What is it?"

""Well, I polled our contacts at Visa, Master Card and American Express. Two days ago, somebody used David Raintree's credit card for a room at the Sea Breeze Motel. It's a place out on Danforth Avenue, near Brimley."

"I know it. It's a low rent passion pit where hookers take their johns. Great work, Sam. I'll go over there right now. I may not be back into the office today, so close up and go home whenever you like."

"I hope you haven't forgotten this Sunday, Matt."

Abruptly, I remembered that it was Friday and I'd agreed to have dinner at Samantha's place on Sunday. I tried hard to think of a last minute excuse, but came up empty.

"I haven't forgotten," I said.

"Good. I don't want to keep Tess up too late, so I hope you won't mind if we eat early. Can you be at my place by six?"

"No problem."

"Wonderful. Tess is looking forward to seeing you again. You made quite an impression on her."

"Little girls all like me. Unfortunately, they lose interest when they hit puberty."

"Don't be too sure about that. Bye, Matt. See you on Sunday evening."

NINE

Traffic had chewed up the snow that had fallen earlier in the day, leaving city roads wet and splashy. Some patches of sidewalk still looked as though someone had dusted them with icing sugar. As I drove east on Danforth, the feeble winter sun struggled to break through thick cloud cover, then it gave up.

The Sea Breeze Motel was a single level concrete building constructed around a cracked asphalt parking lot. Pale green paint flaked away from the doors of the rental units, while a flickering orange neon sign displayed the broken outline of a sail boat and a couple of palm trees. The whole place reeked of decay and despair. I parked my Toyota near a door marked *Office* and went inside.

A red faced man with a walrus mustache sat behind the reception counter as he read a copy of *Sports Illustrated*. He looked like a jock gone to seed and dressed the part. His torn hockey sweater and the gray sweat pants sagging from his protruding gut were sad remnants of past athletic glory. When he saw me, the guy put his magazine aside and wheezed to his feet.

"First day's rent in advance, Pal. Cash or credit card only. No personal checks."

"I don't need a room. Just some information."

I reached into my coat, took out the photo of David Raintree his mother had given to me and slid it across the counter.

"Is this man staying here?"

"You a cop?"

"No."

"Then I don't have to talk to you, do I?"

I pulled a twenty dollar bill from my wallet and held it up, folded between the first and second fingers of my right hand.

"I'd really appreciate your cooperation."

My paunchy friend grunted and took the money.

"Yeah, he was here for two nights, but he left yesterday. You're the second guy today looking for him."

"Who was the first?"

"A big cop. Named 'Bick' or something."

"Do you mean 'Beck'?"

"That's it. I'll tell you what I told him. I don't know where this Raintree guy went. He left last night, without even checking out. Tried to stiff me for the room rent, but he won't get away with it. I got an imprint from his credit card."

"Is anyone staying in the room he used?"

"Not right now. Why?"

"I'd like to take a look at the place."

"I got no time for that. Besides, your cop friend looked at it already."

I pulled another twenty from my wallet, hoping it would be enough because it was the last of the cash I had on me.

"Just a quick look," I said, holding out the bill.

"Five minutes, Buddy. That's all. Lemme get the pass key."

The clerk waddled over to a cabinet on the wall and took out a black metal key attached to a brass fob showing the motel's logo. He held the key out to me.

"Unit twenty-six."

I found the unit and opened the door. Inside, the air was as stale as a tomb. I felt around the wall until I found the electrical switch, then turned the lights on and looked around. The place had that standard motel room chic. A drab brown carpet competed with the cheap furniture in an ugliness sweepstakes and the walls boasted fake oil paintings churned out by some factory in Hungary. Here was a room that had seen lots of loveless sex and loneliness.

The double bed had been made up and I heard a faucet dripping in the bathroom. When I opened the bathroom door, I noticed that the cleaning lady had left the light on after she changed the towels. I gave the unit a quick search, but found nothing interesting. As I was about to leave, I noticed a crumpled scrap of yellow paper lying under the small writing table where the telephone was.

I picked up the paper and straightened it out. It was a piece of hotel stationery on which someone had used a ballpoint pen to write "Lawrence Holt" and a telephone number. The note could have been a bit of debris from some earlier motel guest, but I guessed that David Raintree had left it. I put the paper into my overcoat pocket.

After I'd closed the unit's front door and made sure the snap lock had clicked shut, I walked back to the motel's reception office.

The paunchy desk clerk was back behind the counter, lost in his magazine again. He barely looked up when I put the room key onto the counter.

"Did Raintree make any phone calls?" I asked.

The fat guy looked up at me with a bored expression.

"A couple of them. Just local calls. We don't track those because we don't charge for them."

"Thanks," I said and walked toward the door.

"Hey," he called after me. "What'd this guy do anyway?"

"He killed Santa," I said. "Rudolph is really pissed about it."

I got into my car, started the engine, then drove out onto Danforth and headed west. By now, it was late afternoon and the day had shrunk down into the kind of gloomy twilight that's the curse of northern winters.

Rush hour traffic was building and the sidewalks were filling up with people slogging home from work. Wearing their salt stained parkas and boots, they looked like a tribe of Inuit headed for a new hunting ground.

Off to my right, I saw a forlorn looking Salvation Army officer huddled in a doorway and stamping his feet to keep warm. He kept his lonely vigil near a glass Christmas donations kettle with a bright red ribbon bow tied to it. It was hard to be sure from a distance in the fading light, but it seemed that his kettle was

almost empty.

I'm not sure when I realized I was being followed. At first, I had just a vague sense of uneasiness without knowing the cause. After a while, I realized I'd made a few turns from one street to another on my way home, but the same black Lexus sedan was always back there. I thought about trying to shake off my pursuer, but traffic was congested and I wasn't in the mood for games.

When I stopped for a red light, the blue and white plumbing supplies van behind me turned off into a strip mall. That left the black Lexus in full view of my car's mirrors. I saw that the driver was a grim faced man with a shaved head who wore a navy pea jacket over a red turtle neck sweater. He was nobody I'd seen before.

While I waited for the light to change, I pulled a pen and a notepad from the Toyota's glove box and wrote down the license number of the Lexus. I've got a contact in the motor vehicle registration office who runs plate checks for me, provided I grease his palm with enough cash. Most likely, I'd find out the Lexus had been registered under a phony name or wore stolen plates. Still, I might get lucky. Who knows?

I didn't want my pal in the black sedan to follow me home. When I saw a shopping center ahead, I turned right at the entrance and drove in. After I parked my Toyota in front of a shabby supermarket, I looked back and saw the Lexus stop just a few parking spaces behind me. My tail wasn't being very subtle.

I opened my car's glove compartment. I keep a small gun rack inside that holds a Glock 26 semiautomatic and some ammunition clips. I prefer to work without carrying a gun, but I try not to be stupid either. If my buddy in the Lexus was armed and decided to get nasty, I didn't want to be caught like a nudist at a fashion show.

I shoved the Glock into the right hand pocket of my overcoat before I got out of my car. Keeping my hand on the pistol, I walked back toward the Lexus. I planned to ask the bald guy whether he worked for Kursov or for Beck. It didn't happen that way. When he saw me coming toward him, my shadow started his car's engine and drove away. I guess following me was no fun any more, now that I knew about it.

TEN

I floated blissfully in warm darkness until I heard muted voices from somewhere. Because I was happy in my oblivion, I ignored the voices but the voices wouldn't go away. Instead, they became louder and more demanding.

"Traffic on Highway 401 is just crawling along," said one voice.

"Minus five degrees Celsius at Pearson Airport," a second voice added, as though that was important information.

"Go away," I muttered, then I opened my eyes.

My clock radio had come on, tuned to an all news and weather station. I groaned, then sat up and put my feet over the edge of the bed. It was Sunday, but I had things to do anyway.

Dimly, I can remember when I was much younger. In those days, I woke up ready for whatever life threw at me. Now, it takes longer and longer to pull myself together in the morning. I used to believe that age would at least bring wisdom and serenity. Now, I know it just brings arthritis.

After I used the toilet, showered and shaved, I felt less like a cadaver. I wolfed down some breakfast and was sipping contentedly on a cup of Chinese green tea when the phone rang. I told myself to ignore it. It was Sunday and I needed my weekend. Unfortunately, I never listen to me. Still wearing just boxer shorts and slippers, I padded over to the phone.

"Hello?"

"Have you found my son, Mr. Ryan?"

"No, Mrs. Raintree, but I know he's alive."

"Thank God! Where is he?"

I gave her a brief summary of my trip to the Sea Breeze Motel.

"I don't understand," she said. "Why would David be staying in a place like that? Is he in some sort of trouble?"

"That's what I'm trying to find out."

"Mr. Ryan, I called because I've found something that belongs to David."

"What's that?"

"His computer. It's one of those little ones you can carry with you. 'Notebooks' I think they're called. David usually takes his to work, so I didn't expect to find it here. It was at the back of his bedroom closet. Should I give it to the police?"

"No. Let me look at it first. There may be some information on it that will help locate David. Mind if I come over and get it from you this morning?"

"Of course not."

"Good. I'll be there in about an hour. Thanks for calling."

"Mr. Ryan, I want you to find David soon."

"I'm doing my best, Ma'am."

I hung up the phone and concentrated on dressing. Whenever I call on big money, I try to spruce myself up a little. After scouring my clothes closet, I managed to find a clean shirt and a necktie that wouldn't glow in the dark. I picked my gray suit because it had fewer wrinkles in it than the blue one. Finally, I loaded my pockets with the wallet, car keys and other junk that I tote around with me like The Ancient Mariner's albatross.

On my way to the door, I stopped at the chess board I've got set up on my coffee table. Long ago, I accepted the fact that I'll never be any good at chess, but I like the game. It distracts me during those long stretches when depression presses down like a cold, wet shroud and I want a shot of booze more than anything else.

I'd set up the pieces on my board to replay one of the classic games by the great Jose Capablanca. I glanced at my chess book, studied the board for a minute and then moved one of my knights. Capablanca didn't make a counter move right away. Being dead had slowed his game considerably. I decided not to wait for him and I went out.

Outside, the sunshine lifted my spirits, but it offered little warmth. I buttoned my overcoat tighter against a northeast wind that cut like a razor blade. I rent a one bedroom apartment on the fourth floor of a low-rise building in North York. The place is clean and well maintained, but doesn't have luxuries like an indoor parking garage. My Toyota had been sitting out all night in the cold and the engine growled sluggishly when I turned the ignition key. Finally, the car did start and I was ready to go.

I put on my sunglasses, then tuned the car radio to a local jazz station. Coleman Hawkins and Miles Davis were locked in a duet as I drove out of the parking lot and headed for the Don Valley Parkway. Sunshine and jazz. Life was good. Five minutes later, the music was interrupted by a weather forecast.

"Enjoy the nice weather while you can," the announcer said. "Snow will move in tonight and we may get twenty centimeters of the white stuff before it's over."

I switched the radio off. The weatherman had certainly managed to rain on my parade. Or snow on it. I concentrated on steering my Toyota through the city traffic until I was in Rosedale.

The Raintree house looked less forbidding on a sunny day, but still held a trace of its Victorian gloom. Mrs. Raintree came to the door within a minute after I rang the bell. She wore a black dress with silver piping on the cuffs. Since the last time I'd seen her, dark circles of worry and fatigue had formed under her eyes.

"Come in, Mr. Ryan. I apologize for the mess. My housekeeper Beatrice is sick today."

I looked around and decided I'd seen museums in greater disarray than this house.

"I'll just take the computer and be on my way, Mrs. Raintree. Try not to worry. I'll find David."

She nodded and I felt guilty because I wasn't nearly as confident as I pretended. While I waited at the door, she went back into the house, then she returned carrying a slim notebook computer packed into a black nylon tote bag. I thanked her, then took the computer back to my car and stowed it in the trunk. When I got home, I planned to comb through all of the files on the hard drive, looking for some clue to what was going on. I hoped that David Raintree was as careless about data security as most people are, so he wouldn't have used encryption or access passwords to protect his data.

Back at my place, I parked the car, took the notebook out of the trunk and rode the elevator to the fourth floor. I was about to unlock the door to my apartment when I noticed that it was already slightly ajar.

I went back down to my Toyota, put the computer back into the trunk and retrieved my gun from the glove compartment. When I got back up to my apartment, I held the pistol in a firing stance and kicked the door open. What I saw looked like the aftermath of a tornado. Clothes, books and papers were strewn around everywhere. Staying close to the walls and keeping my gun ready, I moved from room to room. The place was empty. The people who did this must have seen me go out and decided to toss the place before I got back.

I was grateful that the intruders had picked the lock rather than smashing it. After a couple of hours of cleaning up, I had most of my stuff stowed away again and there was less damage than I'd feared. Nothing seemed to be missing, but I wasn't surprised about that. I doubted this had been a conventional robbery. Somebody had been looking for something very specific.

I guessed that some of Kursov's men were responsible for the break in. If the cops had done an illegal search, they'd have been more careful about not leaving signs of it behind. This had been a crude job and I suspected that my buddies Ivan and Victor were responsible. Those two guys were really starting to annoy me.

ELEVEN

After I fixed a cup of hot chocolate for myself, I plugged in David Raintree's computer and booted it up. Fortuntely, David was as ignorant about security as most people. A screen popped up right away, demanding a user name and password. Holding my breath, I typed in "david" for the user name and "raintree" for the password. Bingo! All files were visible and open for access. Very tricky, David.

For the next two hours, I combed through Raintree's documents and email messages. I found letters, draft contracts and a few legal briefs about civil cases. Any of them would be a potent cure for insomnia. None showed any reason for the guy to run away, except to escape terminal boredom.

I was about to shut the computer down when I discovered a small text file stored in one of the folders for David's word processor program. The file consisted only of nine words, typed in capitals: *WE HAVE TO PAY FOR WHAT WE HAVE DONE.*

A light bulb went on inside my head. David Raintree hadn't received the message his mother had showed to me. He'd sent it. To whom? Why? This case was beginning to make me feel like a man who started wading cross a shallow stream, only to find himself sinking into quicksand.

So far, I knew three things. First, some newspaper story about renovations at David's old school had pushed him from eccentricity into full blown craziness. Second, Sergeant Beck was more interested in David than he pretended. Third, Yuri Kursov wanted something belonging to Eric Weisman and thought I might have it. Those were some of the pieces of the puzzle. Somehow, I had to figure out how they all went together.

When I looked at my wristwatch, I saw that it was four o'clock. I'd promised Samantha I'd be at her place by six. After switching the computer off and stowing it away, I took a shower, changed my clothes and shaved again. I felt as nervous as a teenager getting ready for the school prom.

By the time I drove my Toyota out of the parking lot, the dark sky had clouded over and the air temperature was rising slowly. During a Canadian winter, those two things together usually mean snow is coming. I hoped the bad weather would hold off until morning because I didn't relish the idea of driving home later in a storm.

Deliberately, I took a few wrong turns on the way to Samantha's house, while checking my car's rearview mirror for signs of pursuit. If people were shadowing me, I didn't want to lead them to Samantha and Theresa. So far as I could tell, I wasn't being followed.

Samantha had a small brick bungalow in the kind of working class Downsview neighborhood where homes contain more bowling trophies than books. Samantha told me once that her husband Paul hadn't left her much more than the house and the mortgage payments when he died. That was why she had to take any job she could find, even one working for someone like me.

As I steered my Toyota into the driveway, I saw that the house's front porch lights were on. I locked my car, walked up the concrete front steps and rang the bell. After about thirty seconds, Theresa opened the front door. She wore a green and white dress that went well with her red hair and she looked more grown up than her years. Theresa was going to be a real heartbreaker when she got older.

"Hi, Mr. Ryan. Please come in."

I stepped into warmth of the hallway.

"Hello, Tess. My name's Matt. Remember?"

I saw Samantha standing in the hallway, a few feet behind her daughter. Her body was silhouetted against the light and her turquoise dress showed off her figure in a way that made me hope I wasn't staring.

"Did you bring me anything, Matt?" Theresa asked.

"Tess!" Samantha said. "That's terrible. Don't be so rude."

"It's all right, Sam. As a matter of fact, I do have something for you, Tess."

I reached into the left pocket of my overcoat and pulled out a small package wrapped in bright red tissue paper. I bowed before I gave it to Theresa.

"Thank you very much, Matt," she told me solemnly, looking sideways at her mother as if to say, "See, Mommy, I do have manners."

I watched while Theresa tore open the package. I've no clue about shopping for little girls, so I'd picked out almost the first thing I could find. I hoped a nine year old girl wouldn't find my gift too square and corny. Theresa ripped away the tissue paper to reveal a small blue box. Inside, she found pair of faux ruby earrings, the kind a much older girl might wear. I heard her gasp and I knew I'd made a lucky guess.

"They're beautiful," Theresa said.

She threw her arms around me and pressed her head against my waist.

"Thank you so much, Matt."

I began to feel embarrassed.

"Finish setting the table, Tess," Samantha said. "I want to talk to Matt."

Theresa made a pouting face, but she put the earrings into a pocket of her dress and went off down the hall.

"You're going to spoil her," Samantha said to me.

"I don't expect to see Tess often enough to do that. You should be able to offset my corrupting influence."

"Don't you think those earrings are a little grown up for her?"

"When girls are very young, I buy gifts that imply they're older. As soon as they reach twenty-five, I reverse the process."

Samantha laughed.

"You think your Irish charm can get you out of anything, Matt. I'm serious. Tess is growing up so fast it really scares me."

"You and every other mother who has a daughter. I'm sorry if my present wasn't appropriate. I meant no offense."

Samantha gave me a look that I couldn't read.

"I can't imagine you being offensive, Matt. Anyway, it was really sweet of you to think of Tess."

Before I could say anything, Theresa came back down the hall, wearing a frilly white white apron over her dress.

"Everything's ready, Mommy."

"That's good, Honey. Let's all go into the dining room."

We ate roast pork, rice and a tossed salad. For me, it was a treat to have a home cooked meal. I can prepare something basic for myself, when I have the time, but I'll never be considered a chef. Afterwards, Samantha served fruit flan for dessert and I sipped a cup of coffee while I wondered where the evening would go from there.

Theresa left the dining room for a few minutes to brush her teeth. When she came back, she carried a pair of video game control units.

"Want to play *Asteroid Explorer* with me, Matt?"

"Maybe I should help your mother with the dishes."

"I'll be fine on my own, Matt. Go ahead and play the game with her."

Hopelessly betrayed, I played four sets against Theresa. She beat me easily every time and it obviously delighted her. Finally, we abandoned *Asteroid Explorer* to switch the TV set on and watch some silly situation comedy. I fought to keep awake while Theresa giggled all through the program, confirming my suspicions about the target age for most television programs.

As I sat there on the sofa with Theresa snuggled against me, I realized how different this was from the way I usually lived. I guess some people are destined for domestic bliss. The rest of us only get to watch from the outside.

Finally, Samantha came back from the kitchen. She looked at her wristwatch and frowned.

"Tess, it's ten-thirty. You should be asleep."

"Oh, Mommy! Can't I stay up a little longer?"

"No. You have school tomorrow. Now, go upstairs and get ready for bed. I'll come up in a few minutes to tuck you in."

Theresa made a sour face, but knew when to accept defeat. She put her arms around me and gave me a hug.

"Good night, Matt. I'm so glad you could come over."

"Me too," I said, caught off guard.

Theresa turned and went upstairs. Samantha had accused me of relying on charm, but I could take lessons from her daughter.

"More coffee, Matt?" Samantha asked.

"Just half a cup, thanks."

Samantha sat down next to me on the sofa. We sipped our coffee for a minute without talking, then Samantha put her cup down on a nearby end table and looked at me.

"Tess really adores you, Matt. I've never seen her take to anyone so quickly."

"She's a wonderful little girl, but she's a poor judge of character."

"You're not so bad."

"Maybe you just don't know me."

"That's my problem. Despite all the time I've worked for you, there's quite a lot I don't know."

"Such as?"

"Well, for example, have you ever been married?"

"For seven years."

"I guess I shouldn't ask what happened."

"You just did. Jane and I were happy at first, but my job has weird hours. She got tired of staying up nights and worrying."

"Any woman who marries a cop or a fireman has the same problem."

"Some women can handle it, Sam. Others can't. There was something else too. The stress of my job caught up to me and I started drinking too much."

"I've never seen you take a drink, Matt."

"I've been clean for three years now. Anyway, I don't blame Jane. She lives out in Vancouver now. If I'm lucky, I get a card from her at Christmas."

"Did you and Jane have children?"

"No. Considering what happened to our marriage, that's a blessing."

Samantha moved closer to me and put her hand on my arm.

"Don't you ever get lonely, Matt?"

I thought about the days when just making it to sundown was an achievement and sleepless nights that dragged on forever. Lonely? Not me.

I was going to say something, but I looked at Samantha's face and thought I saw an invitation. Leaning forward, I kissed her on the mouth. Samantha pulled away. *Well, Ryan, you've just made a fool of yourself again.*

"I'm sorry, Sam. That was way out of line. It won't happen again."

Samantha looked at me and smiled.

"Are you sure,?" she asked, then gave me a long, lingering kiss.

"I'd better go," I said.

"You can stay here tonight," Samantha said as she stroked my cheek with her fingers. "But you'll have to leave leave early tomorrow, before I get Tess up for school."

Common sense told me that getting sexually involved with my assistant would be a huge mistake. I saw Samantha's lovely face in the lamplight, her lips slightly parted, and caught the fragrance of her perfume.

"I'll leave as early as you like," I said.

TWELVE

When I left Samantha's house around seven the next morning, it was still dark and snow was falling. I kept my Toyota in second gear and drove very slowly because the car's headlights barely pierced the white wall swirling around me.

By the time I reached my street, the roads were covered by a thick white carpet and driving was a treacherous business. At one intersection, I'd seen a black Ford SUV slide into the rear end of a silver Mazda that had stopped ahead of it. Before the storm blew itself out, there would be hundreds of fender benders like that one. I felt a surge of relief when I parked my Toyota in the lot behind the apartment building where I live.

My gray tweed overcoat was caked with snow by the time I crossed the parking lot to the building entrance. I went into the foyer, stamped my feet to shake some snow from my shoes and then rode the elevator to the fourth floor. As soon as I was inside my apartment, I picked up the phone and called Samantha's number. I felt a strange surge of euphoria when I heard her voice.

"Hello?"

"Sam, it's Matt. I got home all right, but it's really ugly out there and the roads are bad. I don't plan to come into the office today. No need for you to be there either. Stay home and keep safe."

"What if a client comes in?" Samantha asked.

"I don't have any appointments booked and I doubt anybody will just drop in on a day like this. What will you do about getting Tess to school?"

"I just caught the weather report on the radio. They say we'll get at least fifteen more centimeters before it's over. The school bus Tess rides has been canceled for the day. I'm going to keep her home with me. What will you do all day, Matt?"

"I plan to call Eric Weisman's sister. I've been told she and David Raintree are a couple. Maybe she knows where he's hiding. "

"You're going to drive in this storm? Traffic will be terrible."

"Weisman's sister lives downtown, near the University subway line," I said. "My place is just a few blocks from the Don Mills Station. I'll walk over there and take the train downtown. I'll be warm and dry, riding below all of the mess at street level."

Samantha and I were both silent for a moment. We were thinking about the same thing, but neither of us wanted to be the first to mention it.

"About last night ...," Samantha said. "I hope you don't think that I usually ..."

"Last night was wonderful, Sam. What happened was as much my idea as yours. Let's just treasure the memory."

"You make it sound as though we'll never do it again."

"I didn't mean it that way. We'll talk about it tomorrow. Okay?"

"All right, Darling."

I hung up the telephone, aware I'd become that oldest of locker room jokes, the boss having an affair with his secretary. Suddenly, I remembered something else. Because of staying overnight at Samantha's place, I'd forgotten to take the little blue pill that keeps my world from falling apart. Missing one dose might not matter, but I'd have to be careful not to miss another. Otherwise, I'd take a trip back to Hell when the residue of the drug in my body dropped below the critical level.

In an effort to busy myself with work, I looked up the phone number of Weisman's sister. She was listed in the White Pages as "Dr. S. Weisman". When I called her home number, she picked up after three rings. Somewhere in the background, I heard a radio or a stereo playing the overture from *Swan Lake*.

"Hello?" She had the kind of sultry female voice that keeps the telephone sex industry so profitable.

"Good morning, Dr. Weisman. My name is Matt Ryan and I'm a private investigator trying to locate David Raintree for his mother. I'm told you know David and I'd like to talk to you about him."

"David's missing? Are you sure?"

"His mother hasn't seen him in a week."

"My God! Rebbecca must be frantic. It's not like David to stay away from her. What makes you think I'd know where he is?"

"You may know something about his habits or you might remember something he told you. Can we meet for lunch and talk?"

"Sorry, but I have a lunch date already. It's just eight-thirty in the morning right now. Can you be here within an hour?"

"There's a storm going on, but I'll do my best."

"Good. I'll tell the security guard to expect you. See you later, Mr. Regan."

"It's Ryan. Thanks very much, Dr. Weisman."

I put the phone down and went to my closet. After hanging up my wet tweed overcoat, I put on a chocolate brown parka with a storm hood and pulled shoe rubbers over my black oxfords. There was no time to prepare any breakfast. I'd have to grab a cup of coffee and a muffin on my way downtown. I locked my apartment, rode the elevator down to the lobby and stepped out into a curtain of roiling snow driven by a bitterly cold wind.

Before I started for the subway, I went to my car and retrieved my Glock from the glove box. I felt better after I shoved the pistol into the right pocket of my parka. People were starting to play very rough games and my little 9mm friend was going to be with me from now on.

As I walked along Sheppard Avenue, lines of cars crawled through the snow, their drivers trying not to skid on the greasy pavement. The morning rush hour was underway by now. Compared to the roadway, the sidewalks weren't very crowded. I saw a group of morning commuters huddling against the wind in an ice coated bus shelter located across the street. They looked so cold and miserable that I felt sorry for them.

It's amazing how snow can muffle noise. Except for the rumble of an occasional passing snowplow, the streets were fairly quiet. For a while, the world was covered by a beautiful blanket of white. City traffic was already converting the pristine snow into filthy, oil soaked slush. Man soils everything he touches.

When I looked behind me, I saw a dark figure moving through the swirling whiteness. It was the bald guy who'd followed me in the Lexus. He'd traded his navy pea jacket for a forest green parka, but I still recognized him. I stopped walking and my buddy did the same as he stared into the window of a Tim Horton coffee shop, pretending to have no interest in me. He was really lousy at tailing people.

I ignored him and walked on until I passed the doorway of an office building that threw a dark shadow. Leaving the sidewalk, I hurried into the doorway, pressed myself against one wall and waited. A moment later, the bald man came along, walking quickly and peering around as he tried to find me. I stepped out of the doorway and smiled at him.

"Nice day," I said.

Startled, the bald man shoved his right hand into the partially unzipped front of his parka. I knew he wasn't reaching for a Kleenex. He stopped when he saw my Glock pointed at his chest.

"Let's not do anything hasty," I said. "Are you working for Beck or for Kursov?"

The man glared at me in sullen anger.

"I not understand," he said in a thick Russian accent.

"Thanks. You've answered my question. Tell Mr. Kursov to have a nice day. Now, get lost."

The bald man gave me a look of pure hatred, spat into the snow at his feet and then turned to walk away.

THIRTEEN

When I came up out of subway at the Osgoode Station, the snowfall had tapered off and I could see the condominium complex where Dr. Laura Weisman lived. The place was an obelisk of salmon colored marble that towered over the buildings around it. This part of University Avenue once had a certain grimy charm. A pigeon stained Boer War monument shared space with some Art Deco buildings built during the worst of the Dirty Thirties. Now the area is being slowly gentrified, like everywhere else. Greedy developers keep constructing huge sterile filing cabinets for people.

I walked past the condominium's revolving door into an atrium the size of a football field. Daylight filtered in from above through a huge glass skylight, while four bored bronze dolphins preened on a circle of marble pedestals. A gray haired security man sat behind an onyx reception counter, near glass doors that led to the elevators. He was probably redundant because I was sure those doors were locked and alarmed anyway.

The security man looked up at me as I approached his desk. He seemed proud of his powder blue uniform. I handed him a business card.

"Matt Ryan. Dr. Weisman is expecting me."

"Got any other identification?" the guard asked in the raspy voice of a heavy smoker.

I showed him my driver's license and he called Dr. Weisman's number to confirm that I was expected. Finally, he made me sign a visitor's register.

"Not bad security," I said.

The guard tried to hide it, but I knew he was pleased by my remark.

"You a cop?" he asked.

"Private investigator."

"Yeah? Well, I spent thirty years on the Toronto force, so I learned a couple of things about securing an area. Why'd Dr. Weisman hire a private peeper like you?"

"You were a cop, so you know I'm not going to tell you."

He scowled and then he nodded.

"Must be important to bring you out on a shitty day like this. All right, I'm going to buzz you in. Go to the nineteenth floor. Turn left when you step out of the elevator and you can't miss the place."

"Thanks. By the way, did you know a Sergeant Joe Beck when you were a cop?"

"I knew him. You a friend of his?"

"No."

"Good. The guy's a king size prick."

When I got off the elevator on the nineteenth floor, I turned left and walked down a corridor boasting silver wallpaper and a chocolate colored carpet. At the end of the hallway were two white doors bordered with navy blue. I pushed the ivory doorbell button next to the left hand door and waited. A moment later, the right hand door opened and I saw a young black woman wearing a lime green dress.

"Mr. Ryan?" she asked.

"That's right."

"Please come in. Dr. Weisman will see you in a minute."

I stepped inside, trying to hide my amusement. So, Dr. Weisman was a rich white woman who had a black maid. It was so banal that it was funny. I had no idea I'd come here to interview Scarlet O'Hara.

"May I take your coat?" the young woman asked.

"Thanks," I said as I shrugged my way out of my parka.

"You must be Mr. Ryan," said a sultry voice from behind me.

I turned to see a dark haired woman who appeared to be in her early thirties. Slim and attractive, she wore a crimson jacket with matching skirt and shoes. Her lovely face wore a slightly mocking expression that reminded me of that old time film star Ava Gardner. I could tell from her coiffured hairstyle and designer clothes that she was high maintenance. She walked toward me with a fashion model's poise and extended a cool, slim hand.

"I'm Laura Weisman."

"Hello, Dr. Weisman. I'm very sorry about your brother."

A shadow of pain crossed her face before she regained her composure.

"Thank you, Mr. Ryan. I can't tell you how terrible the past few days have been. Poor Eric was cremated only yesterday. I'm just thankful we had the memorial service before this storm struck."

"May I go now, Dr. Weisman?" the black woman asked.

"Of course, Valerie. The weather outside is frightful, so be careful on your way home."

"I will."

Valerie retrieved a gray lamb's wool coat from the same closet where she'd stowed my parka. She pulled the coat on, walked out into the corridor and closed the door behind her.

"Come into my living room, Mr. Ryan. "We can talk more comfortably in there."

The apartment was furnished completely in Art Deco style, with large silver mirrors, black borders and white carpets. I expected Jean Harlow to appear at any minute.

"Please sit down," Dr. Weisman said, pointing at a sofa that had black and white cushions.

I did as I was told.

"You don't look like a private detective, Mr. Ryan."

"Really? How do private detectives look?"

"I expected a crude looking man with a cigar in his mouth. You have a certain air of refinement about you."

"Cigars make me turn green, Doctor. As for refinement, I think I actually read a book once. I just can't remember the title."

"I suppose I deserved that. I meant no offence."

"None taken. Are you giving Valerie the day off?"

"Yes. She needs to study for a commerce exam. She'll be writing her Christmas term papers at university next week."

"I guess the bar has been raised for domestic help."

"Now who is thinking in stereotypes, Mr. Ryan? Valerie isn't my maid. She's my executive assistant. She handles my appointments, my correspondence and my finances. I don't know what I'd do without her. Now, why did you want to see me? You said something about David Raintree being missing."

"For a little over a week now. I know he's still alive because he was seen at a cheap motel only yesterday. David's mother wants me to find him, but he doesn't want to be found. One of his co-workers at the law firm told me you've been there with him often. Are you and David romantically involved."

"What?"

She began to laugh. I had to admit it was a nice laugh.

"That's just too funny, Mr. Ryan."

"I guess I missed the joke. Could you fill me in?"

"Well, to begin with, David is gay."

"I don't remember his mother mentioning that."

"Even these days, it's something Rebecca would hardly want to advertise. Wait here for a moment. I want you to meet someone."

Dr. Weisman left the room while I sat there and looked at a color photograph mounted on the wall across the room. It was a picture of a beautiful young woman who was lying in a hammock. She was nude, but she'd been posed with her hands covering the most interesting parts. I'd just conjured up a pleasant fantasy about the two of us when Dr. Weisman returned from another room. She had a man with her.

The guy was tall and good looking, with blond hair and the kind of dark tan you don't get in Toronto during winter.

"Mr. Ryan, this is Larry Holt. He's just back from Cuba. Larry and I are engaged to be married."

Holt shook my hand with a grip that could crack walnuts.

"Laura tells me you're a gumshoe, Ryan."

"I like the word 'investigator' myself."

"Mr. Ryan thought I was David's girlfriend."

"That's rich," Holt said. "I doubt David has ever even kissed a woman. Teenage boys are more his speed."

Holt gave a braying laugh in appreciation of his own remark. Now that I was meeting Raintree's friends, I began to understand why the guy wanted to get away.

"How long have you both known David?"

"Larry and my brother Eric went to school with him. They were together so much that people called them 'The Three Musketeers'. Didn't they, Larry?".

"Yeah. We were tight in those days."

"At The Shawncrest Academy For Boys?" I asked.

"You've done your homework, Ryan."

"Did anything happen while you were at school?"

"Happen? What do you mean?"

"One of David's co-workers told me David got very upset when he saw a newspaper story about the school. Maybe it brought back some unpleasant memories."

"It was probably nothing. David has always been high strung."

"Received anything unusual in the mail lately?" I asked.

"Not really. Why?"

"You did get one thing, Larry," Dr. Weisman said. "Remember the note I found on your desk at the office last week? It was just the strangest message."

"Did it say 'We have to pay for what we have done'?" I asked.

"My God!" Dr. Weisman said. "How did you know that, Mr. Ryan?"

"I think David sent that message, but I don't know why. Any idea what it means, Mr. Holt?"

"Search me. Lately, David's been acting even weirder than usual. Maybe he's having some kind of breakdown."

"Maybe," I said. "Does the word 'hangman' mean anything to you?"

Holt caught himself quickly, but I saw a look of stark fear on his face for just a second.

"Not a thing. Should it?"

"The word was written in ... was found at the scene where Dr. Weisman's brother died."

"Sorry, but I can't help you with that."

Dr. Weisman gave me a look that told me the interview was over.

"Larry and I were about to go shopping and then to lunch. I know the streets are a mess, but we'll use the underground malls. Will there be anything else?"

"Not right now. Thank you both for your time."

I left Dr. Weisman's apartment and took the elevator back down to the lobby. One thing I knew for sure was that Larry Holt was lying, but I didn't know why. I nodded to the security guard in the lobby and I was on my way out to the street when I heard Dr. Weisman calling me.

"Mr. Ryan ... Mr. Ryan ..."

She looked shaken up about something.

"My gloves... I remembered that I'd left them in Larry's car, so I went to get them. That's when I saw ... You have to come and take a look at this."

We both got into the elevator and rode down to the parking garage beneath the building. The place was cold enough that I could see my breath and the air reeked of gasoline and tire rubber.

"This way," Dr. Weisman said as she led me to a row of cars parked against one wall of the parking area. "That's Larry's BMW over there."

Larry Holt stood in front of his car, a jet black BMW sedan that was in immaculate condition, except for one thing. Someone had taken a can of blood red spray paint and had scrawled a word across the driver's door in large letters. The word was 'hangman'.

FOURTEEN

Holt trembled as he looked at his car. I could tell that he was angry, but I sensed he was afraid too.

"Goddamn teenage punks!" he said. "I thought you had security in this building, Laura."

Dr. Weisman looked at me as though she hoped I'd defend her against her boyfriend's wrath.

"This was no random act of vandalism," I said. "You were targeted, Holt."

"Really? And what do you know, Ryan? You're just some cheap shit private eye who peeks through keyholes for a living."

"Larry, don't be so rude. Don't mind him, Mr. Ryan. He's very upset."

"I can see that. Better report this to building security and call your insurance agent."

"I know what to do without your telling me," Holt said.

"Why would anyone do this?" Dr. Weisman asked me.

"I have a hunch, but no proof."

I pulled a business card out of my billfold and handed it to her.

"I'll be in touch. Good luck with the car."

Holt muttered an obscenity and waved dismissively. I turned and walked back across the parking garage to the elevators. After I reached the building's lobby, I nodded to the gray haired security guard as I passed his desk.

"What's all the excitement about?" he asked.

"Somebody spray painted a car in the parking garage."

"Shit! I told building management we should beef up access controls on the garage. They wouldn't listen. Now, they'll have my balls for this."

"What kind of security is there now?"

"Mostly smoke and mirrors. People who live here are issued smart cards for access to the garage, but non-residents get in all the time. You just have to wait until a resident uses his card to open the door and drive in right behind him before the door closes again. I wanted entrance barriers and a CCTV monitor at my desk, but managment said those things were too expensive."

I took out the small picture of David Raintree I had in my billfold and handed it to the guard.

"Ever seen him around here?" I asked.

"Maybe. He looks like somebody I rousted this morning, but that guy's hair was a streaky blond. Still, it could've been your boy. He might've used one of those home hair coloring kits you can buy in drugstores."

"What was he doing here?"

"He walked in off the street and just stood around in the lobby, watching the elevators. We get homeless people coming in all the time, so they can panhandle residents who are coming in or out. I don't allow that kind of stuff, so I told this guy to drift. He left without saying a word. You think he's the one who did the car?"

"I'm positive. His name is David Raintree. Are you sure you've never seen him in here before today?"

"Well, he looks a little like a guy I've seen come in with Dr. Weisman, except for his streaky hair and being so dirty and all. How did he get into the garage?"

"Probably the way you described. He waited until somebody drove in and ran inside before the doors came down. He knew the owner of the BMW, so he had no trouble finding it by its license plates. He sprayed painted the car and then hid somewhere near the garage exit until somebody drove out and opened the door for him."

"Now, I'm going to get hosed for a security breach," the guard said. "This will probably cost me my job."

I found my last business card and gave it to him.

"I don't think you should take the fall for this. If you need somebody to testify about what happened, call me."

"Thanks, Man. That's real white of you. Sorry about what I said about private eyes before. Sometimes, my mouth outruns my brains."

"Forget it. I know cops think we're as low as pond scum, but it's a living."

The guard held out a meaty hand.

"Name's Jack Hornsby."

"Matt Ryan," I said, shaking hands with him.

"Think you'll catch this guy Runfree?"

"Raintree. I should have found him before now, but I've been a little distracted lately."

"Yeah. Ain't life a bitch?"

FIFTEEN

By the time that I rode the subway back to the Don Mills Station, the storm was over and the city's snow removal crews were gaining the upper hand in their battle to clean the roads. The weather forecast had been a little too pessimistic and the twenty centimeters predicted had been only ten. By the time I reached home, it was just another gray and messy day in Toronto.

In my hurry to get downtown to interview Laura Weisman, I'd forgotten to grab something to eat. By now, it was eleven o'clock in the morning and I was ready to chew on an old army boot. I let myself into my apartment, made sure that the place hadn't been ransacked again during my absence and then headed for the kitchen.

Breakfast cereal wasn't appealing so late in the day, but I had few other choices in my cupboard and fridge. I found two eggs that didn't look ready to hatch, a can of navy beans in tomato sauce and some whole wheat bread. After scrambling and frying the eggs, I put them onto two slices of the bread and poured some beans over them. The result looked like the aftermath of a bad car accident, but I wolfed it down anyway and loved it.

While I ate, I caught the news on my small TV set. There'd been another gun battle down near The Eaton Center, leaving one person dead and two wounded. The idiots doing the shooting had missed each other completely, mowing down innocent bystanders in their crossfire. More and more illegal guns flood in from the United States every day. Too many of them fall into the hands of dimwitted gangbangers who think their manhood gets enhanced by blowing people away. I switched the television set off in disgust.

Later, I set up the pieces on my chess board and moved some pawns around while I thought about the Raintree Case. At my current rate of progress, Rebecca Raintree would die of old age before I located her son. Somehow, I had to think like David did. Given the messed up state of his mind, that wasn't going to be easy.

David had slipped up only once, when he used his credit card to pay for a room at The Seabreeze Motel. He must have known credit card transactions can be traced, so he was paying cash for things now. There had to be a limit on how much folding money he had with him. Sooner or later, he'd have to go back to plastic or hit a banking machine. Doing either one could blow his cover, so he'd try to stretch his existing cash as far as possible. That meant he needed to find a very cheap place to stay. I thought I might know where that place was.

#

An hour later, I was in Parkdale Village, a half square kilometer area in size in Toronto's west end. Nobody admits it, but Parkdale is a handy dumping ground for people who make us uncomfortable in our trendy downtown restaurants or upscale shopping malls. Newly arrived immigrants, the desperately poor, addicts and the mentally ill all wash up here. Sometimes, they co-exist with a generosity of spirit that we more affluent souls would do well to imitate.

I managed to find a parking space on Roncesvalles Avenue. That's no small accomplishment any day. The mounds of slush pushed to the curb by passing snow plows made it hard for me to position my car close to the curb, but I did the best that I could.

Even down in Parkdale, gentrification is creeping in. A few hipster coffee bars and restaurants have sprouted up among the rows of dilapidated thrift shops, coin laundries and delicatessens that served the neighborhood before.

Two doors ahead of me, I saw an old two story brick building with a hand painted sign outside that read: *Parkdale Drop In Center*. That was my destination.

At the green front door, I dodged a tsunami of slush thrown up by a passing truck and ducked into the building. Inside, the place was warm but dimly lit. In a front room, two emaciated men with greasy hair sat slumped in worn easy chairs while they watched cartoons on a small color TV set. Cooking smells wafted in from somewhere in back. The two guys in front of the television ignored me at first before the older one looked my way. He smiled, displaying a set of rotted teeth.

"Got any smokes, Buddy?" he asked.

"Sorry, I don't smoke," I said. "Is Frank here?"

"In the back," the man said. He turned back toward the TV set. If I wasn't a source of tobacco, I was of no use to him.

I walked down a hallway toward the kitchen area. My nose told me someone was preparing beef stew. A muscular man with a boxer's battered face came out of the kitchen. He wore an apron over his denim work shirt and faded jeans. When he saw me, he stopped and his tough looking features split into a grin.

"Well," he said. "Look what the cat dragged in."

"Hello, Frank," I said. "Smells as though you've finally learned to cook."

"Best stew you ever tasted, Matt, My Boy. Haven't seen you around here for a month of Sundays. To what do we owe this great honor?"

I filled Frank in about the Raintree case, including Eric Weis's murder and then showed him the picture of David.

"Has this guy been around here?" I asked. "He looks a little different now because he dyed his hair blond."

"That guy came in yesterday," Frank said.

"What? Is he here now?"

"No. I offered him a meal and a cot, but our accommodations were a little too basic for him. Before he left, I gave him a list of the rooming houses in the neighborhood. Maybe he rented a place in one of them."

"Can you give me the same list?" I asked.

"No problem, Matt. Want some stew? I think we have enough."

"No, thanks. The list will be enough."

Frank went into another room before coming back with a note pad and a pencil. I waited while he wrote on the top page of the pad.

"Running this shelter is a big change from being a parish priest," I said. "Ever miss the old days, Frank?"

Frank looked up from his writing and smiled.

"Not for a minute, Old Son. When I realized I'd never hit the big time in boxing, I became a priest because I wanted to help people. One day, I realized everybody around me was always talking about Jesus, but nobody paid any attention to what he said. At least, not to the part about helping the poor."

"Jesus would be thrown out of most churches today," I said.

"Yeah. When I began talking about social justice and about how Capitalism wasn't delivering it, my bishop wasn't amused. He told me to stay out of politics and stick to religion. I couldn't see the difference, so I left the Church. Now, I follow Christ in my own way."

"But why here? You've got a university degree, Frank. You could make a good living somewhere and still give money to the poor."

"Why are you a detective, Matt?"

"It's something I know how to do. There are days when I hate it, but I'd rather be doing this than something else."

"You've just answered your own question," Frank said. "Here's your list of rooming houses. Sure you won't have any stew?"

"I'll take a rain check on the stew," I said as I took the list and folded it before putting it into a pocket of my parka. I pulled out my billfold, peeled off two twenty dollar bills and handed them to Frank.

"For the kitchen fund," I said.

"God bless you, Matt. You'll have to drop in more often. Good luck in your search."

"I'll need it," I said as I headed for the door to the street.

#

I spent the rest of the day going from one crumbling rooming house to another, following Frank's list. Nobody in any of those rat traps remembered seeing David Raintree. By the time I went home, I was weary and discouraged. While I stood in my kitchen and brewed a cup of Chinese green, I had a sudden epiphany.

I was wasting my time by running all over town to look for Raintree. I should simply let him come to me. Apparently, David meant to harass Larry Holt about something to do with the word "hangman". All I had to do was to follow Holt and Raintree would show up, sooner or later. As I sipped my tea, I felt much better.

My intercom unit buzzed to indicate that somebody was calling from the downstairs lobby. I walked over to the wall unit and pushed the talk button.

"Who is it?" I asked.

"Matt, it's Samantha."

Surprised, I buzzed her in and went out into the hallway to wait until she stepped out of the elevator. After we were inside my apartment,

I took Samantha's coat and hung it in my closet. She was wearing a burgundy knit dress that clung to her body like a second skin. A Buddhist monk would have been distracted.

"This is an unexpected pleasure, Sam," I said.

"Tess was happy to skip school today because of the weather, Matt. There was no way she was going to miss her ballet class, though. The roads are a lot better now, so I took her over there. Her ballet school happens to be on Leslie Street, not far from here. I have to go back for her in two hours."

"Well, it's great to see you," I said.

"Aren't you going to offer me a drink, Matt? Sorry. I forgot that you don't drink."

"Can't drink," I corrected her. "I can offer you some pretty potent orange juice, if you don't think it will go to your head."

Samantha laughed.

"Orange juice will be fine," she said.

I poured a glass of juice for her and we both sat on my couch.

"I really came over because I missed you," Samantha said. "Did you miss me too?"

"Of course I did."

"Show me."

I put my arms around her and she pressed her mouth against mine.

"Oh, Matt!" Samantha said when we came up for air. "Being with you is so wonderful."

"Sam, you know this could get messy," I said.

"What do you mean?"

"I'm your boss. It's going to be very hard not to let that fact complicate things."

"I'm willing to risk it, Darling."

I decided to be brutally honest and tell her that I didn't want to risk it, but she kissed me again and I forgot what I was going to say. I made one last attempt.

"Sam, the problem is..."

"Matt, I've got less than two hours before I have to meet Tess and take her home. Are we going into your bedroom to make love or do you want to just sit here and talk about your problem?"

"What problem?" I asked.

SIXTEEN

Next morning, I went to my office and started the day by going through the mail. I read three letters from companies selling gizmos they claimed would make detective work a breeze before I tossed each letter into my wastebasket. The firm's monthly bank statement showed that our account balance was a little larger, but still not big enough. Unless I snagged a few more cases soon, I might have trouble paying the office rent, not to mention Samantha's salary.

I turned my mind to less depressing things, such as looking up Larry Holt's home address. If I called Dr. Weisman, she'd give me the information, but that would've been too easy. There were at least two dozen Holts in the phone directory, but only six had "L" as a first initial. I didn't plan calling each of them until I reached the right one. Instead, I ran an Internet search on anyone named "Lawrence Holt" who lived in the Toronto area. I found two, one living in ritzy Forest Hills and the other in Scarborough. My Larry Holt drove a BMW, so it wasn't tough to guess whose address I wanted.

While I thought about my next move, my telephone rang. A flashing green light on the phone told me it was Samantha calling from her desk. I reached out and picked up the receiver.

"What is it, Sam?" I asked.

"There's a Dr. Weisman for you on line one."

"Thanks. Put her on."

"Her voice sounds sexy, Darling. What have you been up to?"

"Sam, just switch me to Dr. Weisman please."

"Yes, Boss."

"Ryan Investigations," I said when I heard Samantha hang up.

"Is this Mr. Ryan?"

Samantha was right about her voice.

"Good morning, Dr. Weisman. What can I do for you?"

"I remembered something that might help your search for David Raintree. Can you meet me for drinks this evening?"

"Why not just tell me over the phone?"

"I'd rather tell you in person, Mr. Ryan. Ever been to Chez Pierre?"

"No, but I know where it is."

"Good. Meet me there at eight o'clock. See you then."

Before I could say anything else, Dr. Weisman hung up. I sat at my desk for a minute or two, wondering what she had up her sleeve. Finally, I stood up and put on my overcoat. I stopped at Samantha's desk on my way out to the parking lot. She looked up from her computer screen and smiled.

"I'll probably be gone for the rest of the day," I said. "If anybody calls, take a message. I'll check in by cellphone."

"I hope you're not off to see Ms. Sexy Voice."

"Jealousy doesn't look good on you, Sam. I'm going to watch a house in Forest Hills. Our boy Raintree has been harassing the owner and he may show up to create some mischief. If he does, I'll be there to nab him."

"Will I see you tonight?"

"Sorry, not tonight. I have to meet somebody downtown about the Raintree case. I'm not sure how late things will go. Give my love to Tess."

"All right., but be careful, Matt. I worry about you."

I leaned down and kissed Samantha on the mouth.

"Here's looking at you, Kid," I said.

She laughed.

"I think I've heard that somewhere before."

"Impossible," I said. "I just made it up."

SEVENTEEN

The city streets were mostly dry by now. Piles of dirty snow on lawns and a few slick side streets served as the only evidence of the previous day's storm. My drive to Forest Hills was uneventful.

Larry Holt's house was a sprawling two story brick mausoleum set well back from the road. It wasn't the kind of place where I'd expect a rich young bachelor to live, but nothing else about the Raintree case made any sense either.

I drove around the neighborhood until I found a side street from where I could see Holt's house, while being invisible to anyone entering or leaving the place. I switched on my Toyota's four way emergency signals before I got out and raised the car's hood. Wealthy people are paranoid by nature. In some place like Forest Hills, a stranger sitting in a parked car would trigger calls to the police almost immediately. I hoped that even the local moguls would pity a poor sod with car trouble who was waiting for someone from his auto club.

After an hour crawled by, watching paint dry seemed exciting by comparison and I began to reconsider my stake-out plan. When I tell myself something I want to hear, it's amazing how convincing I can be. There wasn't likely to be any excitement at Holt's place after all, I reckoned. I'd learned that Larry Holt was a fund manager with *Sunrise Investments*. While I was watching his home, Larry was downtown on Bay Street, busily moving other people's money around. If David Raintree planned any mischief, he'd probably wait until after Holt came home. I'd waste my day watching the house for nothing. With great generosity, I decided to give myself the day off to do a couple of things that I don't get time for often enough.

First, I drove to Jake's Gym, a small Scarborough exercise club that offers a rare combination of reasonable membership rates and clean surroundings. Most of the other club members are cops, firefighters or similar blue collar guys. At Jake's, you won't see any trendy jogging suits and nobody will be doing Pilates. I keep some workout clothes in a locker there.

I jogged around the track a few times, lifted some weights and worked up a sweat. Mostly, I confirmed to myself how old and decrepit I'm becoming. When I'd been humiliated enough, I took a shower and went to the nearby Green Rooster Cafe for lunch. As I sipped the dregs of my tea, I called Samantha on my cellphone.

"Hi, Sam. Anything happening?"

"Mr. Ridley called. He wants to know when you'll have a report about his wife."

I couldn't suppress a sigh. Jack Ridley was a skinny guy who was obsessed by the idea that his wife Audrey was cheating on him. I don't want to be cruel about Mrs. Ridley's looks, but she has a better chance of being abducted by space aliens than of finding a man who thinks she's hot. After following Audrey around for two weeks, I told Jack that his wife was behaving like a nun, but he wasn't satisfied. He insisted that I continue to follow her and I humored him because he kept giving me money. Every now and then, I submitted a report to Jack, telling him nothing had changed. Actually, I think Ridley hoped I'd find Audrey fooling around, so that he'd have an excuse to divorce her. That was his problem, not mine.

"Tell Ridley I'll have something by the end of this week. Anything else?"

"No. Things have been quiet, Matt. How is the house watching going?"

"Fine. I'm just taking a break for lunch, but I have to get back out there."

"All Right. Take care, Matt."

"You too," I said and ended the call.

I felt a little guilty about lying to Samantha as I drove up to Markham and went to *Bull's Eye Firing Range*. I bought an hour of range time and some clips of ammo for my Glock. After I put on a safety visor and ear protectors, I plinked away at some targets. Only a fool carries a gun without practising how to use it. Usually, I can just about hit the broad side of a barn on a good day, but I was on a roll that afternoon. I actually shot a couple of fairly tight patterns. By the time I left the range, my ego was so big it was hard to squeeze it into my car.

From there, I drove home. I'd check my car's rearview mirror every now and then, but I didn't notice anybody tailing me. Either Kursov's men had stopped following me around or they were getting to be better at it. When I got back to my apartment, the fatigue from my workout caught up to me with a bang. I sacked out and slept for two hours.

It was dark outside by the time I got up. I took a shower and then played a jazz DVD while I heated up a frozen chicken dinner. After wolfing down the food, I put on a fresh shirt and a silk necktie to go with my cleaner suit. It was time to go downtown and find out what Dr. Weisman had to tell me.

EIGHTEEN

As I walked up the stairs from the Queen Street subway station, I looked across at Nathan Phillips Square and City Hall. A municipal work crew had put up a giant Christmas tree, just as they did every year. Dressed with colored lights, the lofty evergreen struggled to inject some warmth and cheer into a cold and blustery Toronto night.

Chez Pierre is a fake Parisian bistro located in the lower level of The Sheraton Center, across the street from City Hall. It's the kind of place where management keeps the lights low, hoping you won't notice the small food portions. As I walked in, a tall waiter in a tuxedo came over to greet me. His hair was pomaded down and he had a pencil thin mustache. He looked like a villain in one of those old crime movies.

"Bon soir. Will Monsieur want a table for one?"

The guy was working hard to sound like Maurice Chevalier.

"No," I said. "Monsieur wants the attractive dark haired woman who said she'd meet me here."

The waiter scowled.

"Last booth on the left, Buddy," he said, losing his phony accent.

Laura Weisman saw me as I walked toward her. She stood up and held out her hand.

"So nice to see you again, Mr. Ryan. Please sit down. I'll get us some drinks."

I pulled off my overcoat and sat across the table from her while she waved at one of the waiters. He came right over.

"Bring me a Manhattan," Dr. Weisman told him.

They both looked at me.

"Perrier, with a twist of lime," I said.

The waiter nodded before he headed off to the bar. Dr. Weisman raised her eyebrows slightly.

"Just mineral water? Are you still on duty, Mr. Ryan?"

"No. I'm on bupropion. It doesn't mix well with alcohol."

"That's a medication for depression."

"In my business, who wouldn't be depressed?" I asked.

"Have you tried therapy?"

"I went to a therapist a couple of times. It didn't work out."

"Why not?"

"I decided that I couldn't help him."

Dr. Weisman laughed.

"I'm glad you have a sense of humor, Matt. Do you mind if I call you Matt?"

"Nope. Mind if I call you Laura?"

"Please do."

"Great. Now that we're old friends, what did you have to tell me about David Raintree?"

"You get right to the point, don't you?"

"It's an occupational trait."

"Larry lied when he told you nothing happened while he, Eric and David were at Shawncrest Academy. Something did happen. I think it must have been something terrible."

"What was it?" I asked.

"I don't know. None of them would ever talk about it, but I saw the change in them. Eric was always the life of the party before that. Suddenly, he became moody and withdrawn. Poor David was shy to begin with, but he really crawled into his shell after whatever happened. He started drinking and experimenting with drugs. I guess being gay made David feel even more alone. Larry was the least affected, but even he flies into rages sometimes for no good reason. Something happened to them all right."

"When was this?"

"During their final year at Shawncrest. They were all just sixteen at the time."

The waiter came back with our drinks. Laura sipped at her Manhattan. My Perrier was a little flat.

"You could have told me all that over the phone, Laura."

"I know. I wanted to see you again, Matt."

"Why?"

"You intrigue me. Most men I meet are doctors, lawyers or Bay Street boys. They all act macho, but there's something tamed about them. They don't face danger all the time like you do."

"You've been watching too much television. My job is mostly boring."

"It must get dangerous sometimes."

"Sure, but I survive by being a devout coward."

Laura reached across the table and ran her slim fingers over the back of my right hand. She leaned forward and her face had a dreamy look in the dim light. The pupils of her eyes were slightly dilated and I realized she was a little high on something.

"Joke if you like, but I think you're a little dangerous, Matt. I find that very attractive. I was hoping we could get to know each other much better."

Looking at Laura's lovely face and the way she filled out her dress, I found her offer very appealing. With an effort, I pushed the thought away and lifted her hand off mine.

"What about Larry?" I asked. "Remember him? The guy you're going to marry."

"Larry and I have an open relationship. He doesn't check up on me and I don't check up on him."

"You're going to have a swell marriage. I'm flattered that you like me, Laura. Any man who doesn't find you attractive should have his pulse checked. Unfortunately, I'm involved with somebody and she's not as broad minded as you are."

"I hope she knows how lucky she is," Laura said.

She was slurring her words slightly. Whatever she'd snorted or swallowed earlier was magnifying the effect of the alcohol in her drink.

"Are you all right?" I asked. "I can get you a taxi."

"Don't be silly, Matt. I'm a big girl who can take care of herself. Now, go home if you're not going to be any fun."

"All right," I said as I stood up and put on my coat. "Thanks for the information. Good night."

Laura looked up at me and smiled dreamily.

"I haven't given up on you yet, Matt. You'll come around. I usually get any man I want."

"How nice for you," I said.

On my way out, I found the waiter with the mustache.

"The lady in the booth back there has had too much to drink," I told him. "Better get her a cab."

"She doesn't look drunk to me. We don't tell our customers what to do, unless they make trouble."

"Fine, Genius. She's one of the higher paid doctors in the city. After she leaves here plastered and gets hurt in an auto accident, I guess you won't mind when she sues this joint into oblivion."

The waiter scowled again. I wasn't enhancing his evening.

"Okay, Buddy. You made your point. I'll make sure she gets home all right."

As I left Chez Pierre, I remembered that old saying about virtue being its own reward. Virtue had no other rewards that I could see.

I walked up Queen Street toward the subway station, but I hadn't gone more than half a block before I realized I wasn't alone. Two men came up behind me and a third stepped out of a doorway ahead. I recognized all of them. The guy up front was the man with the shaved head who had been tailing me. The two thugs bringing up the rear were my old pals Ivan and Victor.

NINETEEN

The bald guy nodded to Ivan and Victor and they made a grab for me. I managed to throw a punch that hit Victor's face, but then he and Ivan pinned my arms behind my back. They dragged me into a nearby alley where the only light around us came from one electric bulb screwed into a metal cone over the rear door of a brick building.

The man with the shaved head grinned at my struggles as he reached into a pocket of his parka. When his hand came out, I heard a metallic click and saw the thin blade of a switchblade knife gleam in the light. I tasted the sour bile of fear in my mouth. Being roughed up in a fight is one thing. Waiting helplessly to be sliced and diced by a sadist is completely different. Panic clamped down on my guts as I waited for the first slash of that ice cold blade.

"*Nyet*," said a voice from behind me. The man with the knife scowled angrily, but he put his weapon back into a pocket of his parka.

Yuri Kursov stepped from the street into the alley. He wore a cashmere overcoat that had probably cost him enough to pay a month's rent on my apartment. I stopped struggling when I saw Kursov, but Victor and Ivan still held my arms locked behind me.

"Good evening, Mr. Ryan," Kursov said. "You must forgive my friend Sascha. You have humiliated him twice when he followed you. Now, he wants to carve you up like... I think the expression is 'like a Christmas turkey'. I would let him do it, but it does not suit my plans."

"Three cheers for your plans," I said.

"Always with the insolent jokes, Mr. Ryan. I am almost beginning to like that. Almost. Enough with jokes. I want you to do something for me."

"Is that why your goons have been following me?"

"No. I thought you had something that belongs to me. Now, I do not think so. But you will find this thing for me."

"It would help if I knew what you're talking about," I said.

"Do you know what my business was with Eric Weisman?" Kursov asked.

"I think I can guess. Weisman ran a jewelry business, the type of operation that makes a great front for money laundering. I think you loaned Weisman money to fuel his gambling habit. When he was hopelessly in your debt, you leaned on him to funnel some of your mob money through his business."

"Very good, Mr. Ryan. Anything else?"

"Weisman's sister is engaged to a guy who manages mutual funds. His name is Holt and he doesn't strike me as being a pillar of ethics. Maybe Eric was investing some of your money with Holt, to clean it up even more."

"Excellent," Kursov said, clapping his hands. "You are very clever. Of course, Eric had to record all those transactions somewhere. When he was killed, the police did not find such records at his shop or I would be arrested already. Because you found Eric's body, I thought you took those records. Now, I do not think so. You will find them for me."

"Maybe Eric's killer took them."

"That is for you to decide. You have one week to bring the files to me, Mr. Ryan. If not, your fate will be very unpleasant."

"Why me?"

"Because you are a detective. Finding things is your business, is it not? Now, my men will prove that I am serious about this matter."

Kursov spoke to the others in Russian before he turned back to look at me.

"I have told them not to hit you in the face. Not this time."

Kursov walked back out to the sidewalk and stood under a street lamp. I saw a black Mercedes sedan pull up at the curb and a uniformed chauffeur got out to hold the car's rear door open for his boss. While I watched Kursov's car move away, Ivan kidney punched me from behind.

As I stiffened from the shock of the blow, Sascha saw his chance to hit me in the gut. I sagged to my knees and tasted vomit in my mouth. Ivan and Victor released my arms and let me fall to the ground. While I lay there retching, we all had a game of football. I was the ball. I pulled myself into a fetal position and crossed my arms to protect my face while the three thugs took turns kicking me silly. Once, I managed to roll away from them and tried to get up. While I was still on my knees, they kicked me sprawling again.

I'm not sure how long they kept stomping me, but it seemed like years. I must have passed out at one point. The next thing I knew, I was alone, lying face down in my own puke. If I stayed there on the ground for very long, I'd freeze to death. I saw a garbage can nearby and crawled toward it. When I grabbed hold of the can and tried to stand up, I gasped with pain. It felt as though somebody was jabbing a red hot spear into my ribs. Somehow, I pulled myself to my feet.

I staggered to the mouth of the alley and looked up and down the street, praying for a taxi. I couldn't walk very far in my condition. Everything was blurred and I saw halos around street lights and neon signs. A yellow and black cab stopped on the other side of Bay Street as the driver waited for a red light to change.

Crossing that street was like running the Boston Marathon barefoot, but I lurched toward the cab. I was trying to wave my arms to get the driver's attention, but realized I was flopping around like a drunken penguin. Loudspeakers mounted on the nearby Hudson's Bay Store blared out mechanical Christmas carols. Joy to the world. The last thing I remember was the cabbie's startled face as I fell against the door of his car. After that, I slid down into blackness.

TWENTY

My hospital room bored me. The view from my bed consisted of a salmon pink wall that looked as though it hadn't been repainted since construction of The Great Pyramids of Giza. I wasn't in the mood to appreciate the decor anyway. My whole body ached and pain lanced through me whenever I tried to move.

A pretty young nurse with short dark hair came into the room. She smiled at me, put a thermometer under my tongue and felt my pulse with her cool fingers. I tried to think of reasons to have my pulse checked more often. A moment later, the young nurse retrieved her thermometer from my mouth and studied it as though it held the answer to some great mystery. She smiled at me again and filled a paper cup with water from a blue plastic pitcher that someone had placed on a table near my bed.

"I'm not thirsty," I said.

The nurse pulled a small white pill from a pocket of her greenhospital scrubs and handed it to me along with the glass of water.

"This will make you feel better," she told me.

"Only a bullet in the head will do that," I said.

Still, I swallowed the pill along with a mouthful of the water.

"When can I get out of here?" I asked.

"Dr. Morgenstern will be in to see you soon."

Before I could say anything else, she left the room. I began to feel woozy and slightly nauseous. The symptoms were the same ones I'd experienced when my broken nose was straightened, years ago. Demerol did that to you. I fought to stay alert, but nothing seemed to matter as I floated down into a warm and cozy oblivion.

When I woke up, the pain had subsided a little and Samantha sat next to my bed. Before she noticed I was awake, I saw anguish on her face. She forced a smile when she saw that I was looking at her.

"How are you feeling?" she asked.

"Like The Chinese Army marched over me."

"Are you in pain?"

"Only when I do something strenuous, like breathing."

"What happened to you, Darling?"

"Some people want me to find something for them. They did this to focus my attention."

"Who would do something like this?"

"In my line of work, not everybody I meet is nice."

"Have you talked to the police, Matt?"

"It wouldn't help. There were no witnesses. The guys who thumped me will produce a dozen people to swear they were on the other side of the planet when I got beaten up. How did you find me?"

"The paramedics found one of your business cards in your wallet. Someone from the hospital staff the phoned the office. I was so worried, Matt. I came over here as soon as I could."

"Where are we anyway?"

"North York General. The emergency wards were full at all the others."

"I got lucky. NYG is one of the better hospitals. Not that I plan to stay here for long."

"Matt, you can't leave. You've been badly hurt."

"I have to find something by the end of the week or I'll be hurt much worse. Can you get my clothes?"

"I can, but I won't. Not until you talk to the doctors."

"Then try to get one of them to come in here. What time is it?"

"Four in the afternoon," Samantha said.

"Wow! I've been out for a long time. How's Tess? Shouldn't you be meeting her at the school bus soon?"

"I told Tess you were sick and asked her to stay at school. I'll drive over and pick her up later."

"Better go and get her now. No little girl should be left alone for long in this city. I promise not to leave here until I find out what the doctors have to say."

"If they do release you, how will you get home?"

"I've got money for a cab," I said. "I'll be fine. Can you crank this bed up a little?"

Samantha turned a handle behind my bed's headboard until I was propped up in a sitting position.

"Thanks, Sam. That's much better. You'd better go and get Tess."

Samantha leaned over and kissed me.

"Just get better, Darling," she said.

She collected her coat and purse from a nearby chair before walking toward the door.

"Sam," I called after her.

"Yes?"

"Thanks for coming. It meant a lot to me."

"Me too," she said and left the room.

For a few minutes, I lay there, wondering what to do next. Would David Raintree have any idea who took Eric Weisman's files? Was there a connection between those files and Raintree's strange behavior? If Raintree sprayed the word 'hangman' onto Larry Holt's car, did he also write the same word on the wall in Weisman's blood? What did that word mean anyway? I had millions of questions but no answers. I wasn't even sure that finding the ledger for Kursov would prevent him from killing me anyway, just because I knew it existed.

A slim man wearing round lens eyeglasses walked into the room. He had a dark mustache and hair like a black scouring pad. To me, he seemed a clone of Groucho Marx. Because he wore hospital greens and had a stethoscope looped around his neck, I deduced that he was a doctor. There's no chance of fooling a great detective like me.

"Dr. Morgenstein, I presume," I said.

"It's Morgenstern. Glad to see you're awake. Did you get the license number of the truck that hit you?"

"There were three trucks and they wore shoes."

"Yeah. From the way they marked you up, I can almost tell you what brand of shoes each of them wore. Was this a robbery?"

"No."

"Then what did you do to piss them off?"

"I was late in returning my library books," I said.

"Okay, I get it. It's none of my business. Anyway, the parka you were wearing gave you some cushion against the blows. That's likely the only reason you don't have any broken ribs, but you're badly bruised and there may be some internal injuries. Sometimes, they take a while to produce symptoms. I want to keep you here for twenty-four hours, just in case."

"I don't have twenty-four hours."

"Maybe I didn't make myself clear, Mr. Ryan. You'll be taking a big risk if you leave now."

"I'll be taking a bigger one if I stay."

Dr. Morgenstern sighed. He pulled a pad of paper and a blue ballpoint pen from a pocket of his hospital smock. Using the bedside table as his writing desk, he scribbled something onto the pad, tore away the top page and handed it to me.

"Have your druggist fill this. It'll help with the pain. I'll have the nurse give you a couple of tablets to tide you over until you can get to a pharmacy."

"Will these pills knock me for a loop the way the Demerol did?"

"No. This is just prescription strength ibuprofen. You can take one pill for pain every three or four hours, but no more than four a day. Got that?"

"Got it," I said. "Thanks, Doctor."

"You're welcome, but I still think you're foolish to leave. By the way, there's a Sergeant Beck from the police waiting outside to see you. Want me to send him in now?"

"You called the police?"

"By law, we have to call them whenever we see evidence that someone's been assaulted. Well, I have to make my rounds. I'll send Sergeant Beck in on my way out."

"Sure. Thanks again, Doctor. I'll need my clothes."

"I'll have one of the orderlies bring them to you."

Dr. Morgenstern paused in the doorway and turned back to me.

"One thing puzzles me, Ryan. Usually, when we treat people who've been beaten, they have trauma to their faces. Broken noses, damaged teeth, that kind of thing. The people who attacked you were very careful not to mark up your face. Why was that?"

"Maybe they thought spoiling such beauty would be a crime."

Morgenstern gave a snorting laugh.

"I see they didn't bruise your ego either," he said before he left the room.

TWENTY-ONE

Sergeant Beck shambled into my hospital room wearing a black duffle coat topped by a tomato red scarf. He grunted as he lowered his ample bulk into the same chair that Samantha had used a few minutes earlier.

"You look like shit," he said.

"Careful, Beck. Flattery like that could turn a boy's head."

"What happened to you anyway?"

"I walked into a door."

"Fine. Don't tell me, Smart Ass. See whether I care."

"Why are you here then?"

"Curiousity. One of the hospital guys called in an assault. When I heard the victim was you, I just had to see for myself."

Beck pulled my 9mm Glock pistol from a pocket of his overcoat.

"The paramedics found this on you when they scraped you off the sidewalk. Got a permit for it?"

"Sorry to disappoint you, but I do."

"I don't get it, Ryan. You go around packing heat, but you let somebody use you as a soccer ball. What gives?"

"I was caught by surprise. It won't happen again."

Beck put my gun down on the table beside my bed.

"Who jumped you anyway?" he asked.

"Some Russians."

"Russians? It's been nice knowing you, Ryan. Those guys will kill their own mothers, just to jazz up a boring weekend."

"They didn't want to kill me. They just sent me a little message."

"Better hope they never send you a long letter. Say the word and I'll assign a couple of uniforms to watch your back."

"Your men can't protect me forever, Beck. I've got to sort this out by myself."

"It's your funeral. Just don't say I didn't offer."

"Duly noted. Thanks anyway."

Beck's mouth curled into a satisfied grin.

"Remember how I told you I'd run a background check on you?"

"I remember, Beck. What about it?"

"Well, the Canadian Forces wouldn't tell me anything, so I talked to some guys who were in your old unit."

I knew where Beck was going with this and could see that he was enjoying himself while getting there.

"Why so much interest in my past?" I asked.

"Because I've always thought there's more to you than meets the eye, Ryan. Turns out I was right. Do you remember a Warrant Officer Palischuk?"

"Dimly. I think I met him once."

"He remembers you. Palischuk told me you killed a guy."

"That was an accident."

"I'd love to have a dollar for every time I've heard that one, Ryan. I could retire tomorrow."

"This time, it's true. Want to hear what happened?"

"I'm all ears."

"I was a communications specialist. Codes, ciphers and stuff like that. My unit went to Germany for special training before being shipped to Afghanistan. I was at the bar in a Zweibrucken *gasthaus* when some German guy decided I was checking out his girlfriend. He came over and tried to start a fight about it. The guy was stinking drunk.

I didn't want to tussle with him, but he punched me and I got angry. I swung at him and he tried to step out of the way. He was so sloshed that he lost his balance and fell. His head smashed hard against the brass foot rail under the bar. The German paramedics rushed him to a hospital in Pirmasens, but his skull was fractured and he'd suffered a brain hemmorage. He died while the surgeons were working on him. I never even knew his name."

My fists were clenched hard and I was shaking as I talked. Telling Beck my story brought back the memories that had fueled my nightmares for years. I thought I'd put the incident behind me, but talking about it now was like tearing the scab off an old wound.

"Quite a story," Beck said. "Did you get into shit over it?"

"Of course. The German cops tried to nail me for manslaughter, but my miltary lawyer got the charge knocked down to assault."

"Why even assault? You said the German guy started the fight."

"His friends said otherwise."

"So, you got railroaded, Ryan."

"That's right. It would have been touchy for the Germans to try a NATO serviceman, so I was brought up in front of a military courts martial. They gave me three years in The Glass House."

"What house?"

"Miltary prison."

"Palischuk told me you only served eighteen months."

"Ever been in a military prison, Beck?"

"No. What's the big deal?"

"They pick sadists as guards. Every day, they put you on a work detail and assign an impossible number of tasks. That way, they have an excuse to come down hard on you when you fail to complete them all. Beating prisoners is common, but it never gets reported. One day, I had to run a hundred punishment laps around the prison exercise yard. Half way through, I passed out. In the hospital, the doctors found I was badly dehydrated and had some internal injuries. The miltary brass worried that I might die and cause an inquiry, so they left me alone until I recovered. When I left the hospital, they gave me a dishonorable discharge. That's why I became a private detective."

"I don't get the connection," Beck said.

"Vets call a dishonorable discharge 'bad paper'. When a vet tries to find work, employers always want to know about his servivce record. If you've got bad paper, you don't get hired. I had to take anything I could get, just to eat. One day, I saw a newspaper ad for a skip tracer. The job paid minimum wage, but I learned some tricks about finding people who don't want to be found. From there, I took a couple of courses and got my PI license."

"And lived happily ever after," Beck said. "What about the Raintree case? Getting anywhere with that one?"

"I haven't found Raintree yet, but I think I know what set him off. Something happened to him when he was at that prep school Shawncrest and everything came back to a boil recently."

Beck looked at me intently.

"What makes you think that?" he asked.

"I talked to Laura Weisman, Eric's sister. She told me that Eric went to Shawncrest Academy with Raintree and a guy named Lawrence Holt who is now Laura's boyfriend. Laura said something happened to all three boys at Shawncrest. She doesn't know what it was, but none of them was the same afterwards. I'm going to contact the faculty at the school and find out what I can."

"Why do you care about what happened to them, Ryan? You were hired just to find Raintree and talk him into going home to mama."

"It may be easier to find Raintree if I know what's eating at him. Holt was at Laura Weisman's place while I was talking to her. Raintree sneaked into the parking garage and spray painted Holt's car with the word 'hangman'. That's the same word someone wrote onto the wall on the night Weisman was killed. I think Raintree is tormented about something and he's trying to get Holt involved."

"Do you think Raintree killed Weisman?" Beck asked.

"Maybe. I'm pretty sure he was at Weisman's place on the night Weisman was killed. If David didn't kill Eric, he may know who did."

"It's all a great theory, Ryan, but I don't buy it. Raintree's own mother admits he's been on booze and drugs for years. I think the guy just rotted his brain and flipped out. We've got Weisman's accountant doing an inventory at the jewelry store and I'm betting he finds a couple of items missing. I think Weisman was killed in a robbery."

"Why no signs of forced entry?" I asked.

"Maybe Weisman was dumb enough to leave his shop door unlocked. Maybe he knew the robber and let him in. Who knows? You're welcome to waste your time chasing rainbows if you like. As for me, I've got work to do back at the station, so I'm gonna drift. Try to stay out of trouble, Ryan."

Beck stood up, nodded to me and walked out of the room. Ten minutes later, a thin young hospital orderly arrived with my clothes. My parka and pants didn't look any better after my rolling around on the ground in them. I was able to pull on my boxer shorts, socks and trousers by myself, but I needed the orderly's help to get my shirt on over my bruised torso. The effort of dressing myself left me hurting so much that I was grateful when my dark haired angel of a nurse appeared with a few ibuprofen tablets. I swallowed one right away, along with a mouthful of water.

I noticed the nurse's eyes get big when she saw my gun lying where Beck had left it on the bedside table. I picked up the pistol and dropped it into the righthand pocket of my parka.

"Don't worry," I said. "I only shoot people at parties."

I went to the admittance desk to collect my watch, wallet and other personal effects. After that, I signed myself out and was free to go. In the lobby, I used my cellphone to call a taxi.

The warmth of the hospital lobby was making me sleepy, so I went outside and stood on the hospital's front steps while I waited for my cab. The cold air cleared some of the cobwebs from my brain and the ibuprofen started to kick in, dulling the pain in my ribs a little.

The evening sky was darkening from indigo to black and gusts of icy wind whipped snow streamers into my face. I stood there thinking about my situation. It was about two weeks into the Raintree case. So far, I'd failed miserably to find David Raintree, been threatened by Russian gangsters and beaten to mush. Nice going, Ryan.

I saw headlights flare in the darkness as a yellow and black taxi turned in off Leslie Street and stopped at the curb in front of me. Shivering despite my parka, I stumbled over and opened the rear door of the cab, on my way to whatever happened next.

TWENTY-TWO

I slept badly that night. My bruised body ached badly enough to keep me awake most of the time and I felt like the aftermath of a massacre by morning. On my way to the shower, I caught my reflection in the bathroom mirror and winced. My chest looked like a modern painting done only in black, blue and yellow pigments.

My plan was to go out and beat the bushes again for Raintree. Instead, I spent the day swallowing ibuprofen tablets, putting ice packs against my battered torso and dozing off. By eight o'clock that evening, I'd worked up the ambition to make a phone call.

Fortunately, Laura was home.

"I didn't think I'd hear from you again," she said.

"We need to talk, Laura."

"All right. Go ahead and talk."

"It's something I need to discuss with you face to face."

"Now you're playing that game, Matt. Sure. Come on over."

After I put the phone down, I remembered to check my voice messages. There had been two calls from Samantha, so I tried her home number.

"It's wonderful to hear your voice," Samantha said. "When you didn't answer my calls, I was so worried."

"Sorry, Sam. I slept through most of the day."

"How are you feeling?"

"Like roadkill, but things are getting better."

"Want me to come over?"

"I'll be fine. See you at the office tomorrow. Give my love to Tess."

"I will. Good night, Darling."

I was so sore that I didn't feel like driving my car, so I went downtown by subway. When I reached Laura's apartment building, Jack Hornsby was still working the security desk.

"You again," he said. "How's the gumshoe business?"

"The same as ever. I get my head kicked in for chump change. Don't they let you go home at night, Jack?"

"Usually. Tonight, the kid who should take this shift called in sick. Hung over, I say. At least they gotta pay me time and a half."

Jack called Laura to let her know I was in the lobby before he buzzed me in. I had a brief dizzy spell in the elevator, but managed to get myself under control. When Laura opened her apartment door, she wore crimson silk pajamas. I had to admit that I'd never seen crimson silk looking so good.

"Come in, Matt," she said. "I'm so glad to see you."

Laura took my coat befoe she sat me down on her black and white sofa. The decor of her apartment still made made me feel like an actor in a old movie. When Laura came back from the coat closet, she smiled at me.

"Drink?" she asked. "Sorry. I forgot about the bupropion."

"No problem. Sit down, Laura. I have something to ask you."

She sat close to me on the couch and leaned forward to gently trace a line down my cheek with her right index finger. I caught a whiff of her perfume. It smelled expensive.

"Ask whatever you like, Matt. I'm all yours tonight."

"Your brother Eric was laundering money for the Russian Mafia. Did he keep a ledger to track his transactions?"

Laura's smile vanished and her lovely face became a cold mask.

"Is that what you came here to talk to me about?"

"It's important. The Russians want me to get Eric's ledger for them before the police find it. If I don't have it by the end of the week, they're going to rearrange my molecules."

"Too bad. What makes you think I know anything?"

"Eric wouldn't keep records of illegal transactions at his shop. The cops might show up with a search warrant. He'd want to leave the information with somebody he could trust. A person the police wouldn't suspect. Somebody like you."

"I never got involved with Eric's business. Can't we talk about something else?"

She reached out and tried to unbutton my shirt. I winced in pain when her hands touched my chest. Laura pulled back, puzzled.

"Are you hurt, Matt?"

"The Russians wanted to prove to me that they were serious about the ledger," I said.

Carefully, I undid the top three buttons on my shirt and held the front of it open. Laura's eyes widened when she saw the bruises on my chest.

"Not very pretty, is it?" I asked.

"Oh, Matt! You're getting me wet. I knew you were a man who lives with violence. You don't know how exciting I find this. You poor darling. Here, let Momma kiss it all better."

She lowered her head to kiss my chest, but I pushed her away.

"Aren't you forgetting about Larry? Oh, right. You two have an open relationship."

"Stop talking about Larry. You don't care about him. You don't even like him. You're thinking about that girlfriend of yours."

Laura put her arms around me and kissed me on the mouth.

"I can make you forget that woman," she whispered. "You have no idea how good I can be in bed."

"Sorry, but I'm in no shape for any bedroom gymnastics tonight. I can hardly move."

"That doesn't matter, Silly. There are ways we can do it so that you'll barely need to move at all. You want Eric's ledger? Well, be really nice to me tonight and maybe I'll tell you where it is."

I pushed her off me and stood up.

"All I have to do is be your sex slave, is that it? Maybe you'd like me to wear a dog collar while we get it on. Sorry, but I don't grovel very well, Laura. I'll have to take my chances with the Russians."

"Fine, you rotten bastard! I hope they kill you."

"Maybe they will. While they're taking me apart, I'll tell them you have Eric's ledger. I'm sure they'll come around to chat with you about it."

For the first time since I met her, Laura looked scared.

"You wouldn't really tell them that, would you?"

"Why not? I don't owe you anything. You could save my neck, but you'd rather play games. These guys are really nasty. If they start massaging you with a blow torch, you'll tell them anything, just to stop the pain."

"I don't have the ledger, Matt"

"But you know where it is."

"Larry took it. Eric kept his files on a DVD in a locked writing desk here in my apartment. He wouldn't even let me see them. After Eric was killed, Larry started to worry that there might be something on that disk to incriminate him. He made me give it to him."

I felt a little sick. Larry Holt would have only one reason for taking the files. He wanted to destroy them. They were probably deleted already, but I had to make one last try to get them back.

"Call Larry," I said. "Tell him you want to come over right away, but don't mention the files. Make up some excuse."

"I don't want to get involved in any of this, Matt."

"You are involved. You can either help me to get those files back or you can explain everything to the Russians. You don't want to make the second choice. Now, call Larry."

Laura picked up her telephone and punched in a number. She listened for a minute or two before she turned to face me.

"He's not answering. I'm getting his voice mail."

"All right. Change out of those pajamas while I get our coats. We're going over to Larry's place. Is your car downstairs?

""Yes."

"Good, then you'll drive. I'm too sore."

"If Larry's not home, how will we get in?" Laura asked.

"Trust me. We'll get in. Now, let's go."

TWENTY-THREE

Large snowflakes drifted down as Laura and I drove through the darkened streets of Forest Hills, but the night was mild enough that the white stuff melted as soon as it hit the pavement. When Laura parked her black Volvo in Larry Holt's driveway, we saw the gleam of a single light shining through partially opened drapes on the ground floor.

"Larry must be home after all," Laura said.

"Good. I didn't want to have to resort to burglary."

We left Laura's car and walked up the steps to the front door. As I reached out to ring the doorbell, I noticed that the door was open just a crack and felt the hairs rise on the back of my neck. I'd seen this movie before at Eric Weisman's jewelry shop.

Laura gasped when I pulled my pistol out of my coat.

"My God! What are you going to do?" she asked.

"The door shouldn't be open like this, Laura. There may be trouble inside. We're going in, but be very quiet and stay behind me. Got that?"

"All right. Do you always carry a gun?"

"Only when I expect to need one. Ready?"

"Yea, but be careful. Don't shoot Larry by mistake."

I pushed the front door open and went inside, with Laura one step behind me. The house's large foyer was in darkness, but enough moonlight streamed in through a skylight to let me make out the shape of a spiral staircase on my left. Directly ahead of us, a dark hallway led back into the interior of the building. Halfway down that hallway, a pool of light spilled out through an open doorway. I heard voices, a burst of music and the sound of tires squealing. It had to be the audio from a television set.

Staying close to one wall, I moved slowly down the hall toward the source of the sound. When I was next to the open doorway, I stopped to listen again, but heard only the television blaring. Taking a deep breath, I stepped through the doorway with my gun held in front of me.

It took a second for my eyes to adjust to the light before I saw Larry Holt. He was sprawled against the far wall, his arms and legs flung wide like a rag doll somebody had tossed away. Holt was staring up at the ceiling, but not seeing it. His face was frozen in a look of surprise and there was a bullet hole in his forehead. The slug had gone right through Holt's skull to dig itself into the wall plaster. A bloody smear from the exit wound showed where his body had slid down to the floor.

I saw something else too. Somebody had used Holt's blood to smear the word 'hangman' onto the wall, in block letters. I felt a sick sense of <u>deja vu</u> after finding Eric Weis the same way. On my right, a big screen television set was running some cop show. The killer had probably turned the audio up to cover the sound of the shot. I crossed the room and switched the TV off.

Laura's scream from behind me almost made me jump out of my shoes. She had just seen Holt's corpse.

"Larry! My God! Larry! No!"

She started toward the body, but I caught her left arm.

"You can't do anything for him now," I said.

"He's dead? But how...? Who could have...?"

She fell against me, sobbing. I held her close and let her cry it out. I know how it feels to lose someone you love.

"I need to find those files," I said. "Then we'll call the police."

Laura pulled away and stared at me.

"The files? Is that all you're thinking about with Larry lying there? I didn't know anybody could be that cold."

"Sorry, but, if I don't find that information soon, I may wind up like Larry. I'm sorry he's dead, but nothing I can do will bring him back. If you don't want to come with me, just wait in one of the other rooms. I don't want you to stay here looking at Larry's body. I'll be back in a few minutes."

"No. Don't leave me alone, Matt."

"Let's go then."

With Laura behind me, I began a search of the house. We found a room upstairs that must have been Larry's home office. On top of a large oak desk, I saw a clear plastic caddy filled with DVDs that sat next to a personal computer and printer.

"How was Eric's DVD marked?" I asked Laura.

"With a red label, I think. That one looks like it. Yes, that's definitely Eric's handwriting. Why is the disk marked 'Life Insurance'?"

"A joke," I said. "Eric hoped the Russians wouldn't kill him if he had information to incriminate them. He might have been right. I don't think it was the Russkies who shot him."

I had an uncomfortable feeling because finding Eric's DVD had been much too easy, but I put it into a pocket of my coat before I called 911. Laura and I waited downstairs in the hallway until two uniformed police officers arrived. They asked lots of questions before two grim looking homicide detectives arrived and asked the same questions all over again. I saw Laura shivering and realized how rough this whole thing had been on her.

"May we go now?" I asked one of the two detectives.

A short guy, he scowled and reached out to poke my chest with his right index finger.

"You go when I say you can."

I took him for one of those short men who feel they have to be super tough to compensate.

"I ran a check on you, Ryan," the detective said. "You're one of those candyass private eyes who give us so much trouble. I also know you phoned in another stiff, just about a week ago. Why do people die around you so much?"

"Must be my aftershave."

"Watch it, Smart Mouth. I like taking smart guys down a peg or two."

Just then, Medical Examiner Dr. Paladini walked by on her way to examine Larry's body. She stopped to smile at me.

"Hello again, Mr. Ryan. You'll have to stop bringing me so much business. My staff has more work than they can handle."

"I'll try to remember that," I said.

After she walked away, I turned my attention back to the belligerant homicide detective.

94

"Can we drop the tough guy banter?" I asked him. "We both sound like Humphrey Bogart on a bad day. I'll be glad to come into the station house tomorrow to answer any questions. Dr. Weisman has just found her lover dead and she's uspset. I'd like to take her home now, if that's all right with you."

"Okay, take off. Just don't get any sudden urges to travel."

"Not me. I'm a homebody."

I took Laura by the arm and we started toward the front door. Laura moved like a sleep walker and she wasn't the only one who felt shaken up. I tried not to think about how Larry Holt might still be alive if I'd continued watching his house.

"Please, Matt. I don't want to be alone tonight," Laura said.

"I'll take you back to my place. This time, I'll drive."

"Your place? I'm not sure ..."

"Don't worry. I'll sleep on the sofa bed and you can have the bedroom. Nobody will bother you."

"I'm not worried about that, Matt. I know I can trust you. I just don't want to impose."

"No trouble at all. Give me your car keys. I think you're a little disoriented. Nobody could blame you for that, but you shouldn't drive."

"I am a mess right now. Thanks."

We drove to my apartment through dark and deserted streets. It was after midnight and my bruised ribs were nagging me again. I needed sleep even more than Laura did. After I parked her Volvo behind my apartment building, Laura turned in her seat to face me.

"I can't believe Larry is gone," she said.

"You must have loved him very much."

"That's the strange part, Matt. I'm not sure whether I loved him or not. Larry was just there when I needed him. Despite the cold way he could be with other people, he was good to me. Now, people are dying all around me and I'm not sure of anything anymore. My life is such a mess."

"You just need some sleep, Laura. I know I do."

"Do you think Larry was killed because of those files you have?"

"I doubt it. There was no sign that the killer looked for the DVD. Because of that word marked onto the wall, I think Larry's death is connected to your brother Eric's. I just wish I knew why. Let's go inside now. It's cold out here."

In my apartment, Laura and I talked for a few minutes before I showed her where to find the bedroom and the bathroom. While she went to bed, I pulled spare sheets and a blanket out of my linen closet. After I'd laid out the bed clothes, I stripped to my underwear and turned in for the night. The sofa bed was about as comfortable as a bag of rocks. I was so tired that I fell asleep anyway.

TWENTY-FOUR

Next morning, I crawled off the sofa bed and stumbled into the bathroom for my usual shower and shave routine. When I checked myself out in the mirror, I saw that the bruises on my body looked worse than they had the day before, but they didn't hurt as much. I pulled on a pale blue shirt and gray slacks before sitting down to breakfast.

I'd finished eating and was daydreaming over a cup of Chinese green when I realized I hadn't seen Laura yet. I looked at my wristwatch, walked over to the bedroom and knocked on the door.

"What is it?" she called out.

"It's nearly nine, Laura. Want some breakfast?"

"I'll be out in a minute."

Five minutes later, Laura came out of my bedroom, wearing her clothes from the night before. She went into the bathroom and I heard the shower running. Several more minutes passed before Laura came out again, looking fabulous.

"Good morning," I said. "I can fix scrambled eggs, if you like."

"No, thanks, Matt. I'm not hungry."

I looked at Laura's face more closely and noticed how bright her eyes were. Her cheeks were slightly flushed and her movements were quick and nervous.

"What are you using?" I asked. "Amphetamines?"

"I don't know what you mean."

"Sure you do. You're a medical doctor, so scoring prescription drugs is a piece of cake for you. I'm guessing you jack yourself up on amphetamines in the morning and float down again with Quaalude's or Diazepam at night."

"That's ridiculous."

"Is it? Then you won't mind if I look in your purse."

"All right, Matt. I'm using medication. What of it? My brother and Larry were both murdered Is it surprising I need something?"

"It's more than that. You were high on something back when you met me at Chez Pierre."

"What do you care? You're not my father."

"I shouldn't care, but I do. I hate seeing a beautiful and intelligent woman like you flush her life down the toilet. I know what I'm talking about, Laura. Five years ago, I let everything get to me and I crawled into a bottle."

"It's not like that for me. I'm not addicted or anything."

"That's what I told myself, even after I started having blackouts and got into a traffic accident. My drinking cost me my marriage and my health. I probably had a genetic disposition toward depression anyway, but hitting the booze pushed me over the edge. I don't want something like that happen to you."

"Don't worry about me, Matt. I can stop whenever I want."

"Then stop."

"Lectures about taking drugs sound a little odd coming from you," Laura said. "You swallow bupropion every day, just to keep going."

"All right, I guess I deserve that. Forget I said anything."

"I appreciate your concern, Matt. I really do. You're sweet to worry about me, but I need to work things out by myself."

"Okay. If you don't want breakfast, have some orange juice."

"Thanks, but I have to run. I've got patients who've booked appointments with me this morning and I'm late already. I'll get something at the coffee shop down at the clinic. I promise."

I thought about asking Laura how her patients would feel if they knew they were being treated by a doctor who was buzzed out on speed, but I kept the question to myself. After I walked with her to the door, she leaned forward and kissed me on the cheek.

"Thanks for being there for me last night, Matt. I don't know what I would have done without you. Could I stay here again tonight? I'm still not comfortable about being alone."

"My place is really too small for two people," I said. "There are only so many nights on that sofa bed that I can stand. I could drop by your apartment for a while tonight. On one condition."

"What's that?"

"No drugs."

"Not that again."

"You're more interesting when you're not high, Laura. At least try to stay clean. Just for today."

"All right. I'll try. Will you come over to see me if I do?"

"I will."

"Good. Now, I need my car keys."

"Are you sure you're able to drive?" I asked.

"Of course, Silly. My keys, please."

Against my better judgment, I went to my hall closet and pulled Laura's car keys from a pocket of my overcoat. I gave them to her and she left my apartment. After I finished my tea, I went into the bathroom to brush my teeth. I took a bottle of bupropion tablets from the medicine cabinet and swallowed one of the little blue pills that keep my world spinning. Laura was right. I had no credibility when preaching about drug dependency.

Looking out through my living room window, I saw that it was a sunny day for a change. I collected my wallet, gun, sunglasses and car keys before I left for the office. On my way out, I found the DVD I'd taken from Larry Holt's place and shoved it into a pocket of my overcoat. For the sake of my health, I hoped the disk still contained the data Kursov wanted.

Bright morning sunshine dazzled the drivers on Victoria Park Avenue and slowed traffic as I drove north to Gordon Baker Road. When I finally reached the office, Samantha was already at her desk. She stood up and came over to throw her arms around me.

"Welcome back, Darling. How are you?"

"A little better today. What's happening, Sam?"

"Mr. Cheever called. He's the store owner who thinks that his employees are pilfering his merchandise. He wants your report."

"I told him already that his brother-in-law is the thief," I said with a sigh. "All right. I'll type something up. Anything else?"

"No. I left your mail on your desk."

"Thanks. How's Tess?"

"Fine. She danced in her school play last night and she was wonderful. It's a shame you couldn't be there."

"I'll make it up to her somehow, Sam. Let me dig through the mail before we talk about today."

I walked to my desk and sorted through the pile of envelopes. Junk, junk and more junk. A small yellow envelope caught my eye. It was addressed to me in handwriting I didn't recognize. I used my letter opener to slit the envelope across the top and dumped out the folded sheet of paper inside. When I unfurled the paper, I saw a picture of a brilliant blue butterfly. Underneath the image were the words "Five more days". It was a friendly reminder from Yuri Kursov.

I switched on my personal computer and waited impatiently while the thing took what seemed an eternity to boot up. I got Eric Weisman's data disk from my overcoat and inserted it into the DVD drive. The room turned colder when I tried to read the disk and the operating system told me that it was blank. Goodbye, Ryan.

TWENTY-FIVE

I tried to stay calm as I considered my options. Larry Holt had erased the contents of the DVD to destroy evidence of his involvement with Kursov's money laundering racket. Kursov would never believe the files had been erased, especially with Holt dead and unable to back up my story. The Russian gangster would think I was lying to hide the fact that I'd failed to find the files. He wouldn't be amused.

Going to the cops would be only a temporary solution. The police couldn't protect me forever and the Russian mob would wait patiently for years for a chance to kill me. I could run and change my identity, but that meant spending the rest of my life dreading every knock at the door.

I had only one slim chance, an ex-convict friend named Frank Suzuki. He'd been a computer hacker and he might know how to retrieve at least some data from the disk. If I was lucky, it would be a big enough fragment to convince Kursov that I'd found the right DVD. I decided to call Frank and hope he could save me.

When I looked up, I saw Samantha standing next to my desk.

"You seem worried," she said.

"Just a problem, but I think I can work it out."

"Is it connected with the people who beat you up?"

"Yes, in a way."

"Who were they?"

"The Russian Mafia."

"What? You have to go to the police, Matt."

"That wouldn't help. I have to work this out myself."

"I didn't know your job was so dangerous."

"Sam, you've worked here for over a year. You must have noticed that some of the people I meet aren't very nice."

"I know, but the Russian Mafia? I've heard they'll do anything. Killing you would mean nothing to them."

"Thanks for cheering me up," I said. "Seriously, I don't think they don't want to kill me. Not yet anyway. The Russians just want me to find some information for them. If I do that, I'm hoping they'll leave me alone. Just in case, maybe you and Tess should go away for a little while."

"Do you think they'll come after Tess and me?"

"Probably not. I'm being careful, that's all."

"Tess is in the middle of her Christmas exams, Matt. I can't pull her out of school right now."

"You're right. I guess I'm overreacting. You and Tess will be fine."

"I certainly hope so. By the way, here's something I meant to show you, Matt. I found it shoved under the office door when I came in this morning."

She held out a sheet of paper that had been torn from a lined writing pad. Someone had used a graphite pencil to print a message in large block letters. *I KNOW WHERE YOU WHERE YOU CAN FIND DAVID RAINTREE. MEET ME TONIGHT AT 10 O'CLOCK. THE AURORA GARMENT FACTORY AT 3395 ELLESMERE ROAD. COME ALONE.*

"Do you think this is just a prank?" Samantha asked.

"I don't know, but I'll have to check it out."

"Surely you won't go alone, Matt. It could be a trap."

"I know, but I'll have to chance it. Whoever wrote this will be watching. If I show up with an escort, he'll take off. Don't worry, Sam. I plan to be careful."

"That's what you always say. Look what happened the other night. I worry about you, Matt."

"I worry about me too, but I've got a job to do."

"Does this mean I won't see you tonight?"

"Sure you will, Sam. We'll have dinner before I go out to the paint factory."

"I like the sound of that. What do you plan to do today?"

"I need to see a friend and ask him to retrieve some data that was deleted from this DVD."

"Can I do anything to help?"

"I thought you'd never ask. Scour the Internet for all you can find about The Shawncrest Academy For Boys. Look for any mention of a scandal or an incident that happened there about twenty years ago. Your doing that will help me a lot, Sam. I'm sure there's something about Shawncrest that's the key to this whole Raintree case."

"Aye, aye, Sir. I'll keep the home fires burning while you're out on your sacred quest."

"That's my girl," I said and kissed her.

"Just take me to a nice restaurant this time," Samantha called after me as I headed for the door.

TWENTY-SIX

I had to knock three times before Frank Suzuki opened the door to his apartment. When he saw me standing in the hallway, his dark bushy eyebrows shot up and a grin spread across his Asian face.

"Well, if it ain't Matt Ryan. Haven't seen you in quite a while, Sherlock. C'mon in."

As I stepped into his apartment, I smelled pot smoke. Now, I knew why Frank had been so slow to answer the door. I'd caught him toking and he needed to hide his weed in case it was the police knocking.

Frank's place was a study in clutter, with computer magazines and electronics parts piled everywhere. Half of a pizza still sat in its delivery box on the coffee table, along with a trio of beer cans. Frank brushed a few magazines off the couch and gestured for me to sit there.

"Want a beer, Matt? Sorry, I forgot. You got religion and don't drink any more."

"Fruit juice will be fine, if you have any."

Frank made a face and went into the kitchen. I heard glass clinking and Frank came back with a glass of orange juice. He handed the glass to me and picked up one of the beer cans from his coffee table.

"What's that mick toast you always use?" he asked.

I clinked my glass against his beer can.

"*Sliente*. And don't call me a 'mick'"

"Why not?"

"Most people mean it the way they mean 'nigger'."

"Sorry. No offense."

"None taken. Nice place you have here. It's a long way from that second floor walk up in Ajax."

Frank grinned, sat down in his easy chair and put his shoes up on the coffee table. He still seemed mellow from his pot. smoking.

"Yeah. I was making peanuts fixing computers, but ex-cons like me don't get our pick of jobs. I've got a better gig now."

"Doing what?" I asked.

"Same business you're in."

"Somehow, I can't imagine you as a private investigator, Frank."

Frank laughed.

"Not me, but I work for one. The guy's name is Howard North. Ever met him?"

"No, but I've heard of him. Private investigation is a small pond in Toronto. What do you do for North?"

"Help him with any technical stuff, like recovering data that some dude has tried to delete from his computer."

"Actually, Frank, that's I'm here," I said as I reached into my coat and pulled out Eric's DVD. "Somebody erased the contents of this disk and I'm hoping you can get the information back for me."

Frank took the disk and looked at it closely.

"No sign of physical damage, Matt. That's good because it's really tough when somebody scores the disk or cuts it. I hope your guy didn't use one of those programs that overwrite the data with zeros. Makes it almost impossible to get anything back. What's on here anyway?"

Briefly, I descrbed the Raintree case and my meeting with Yuri Kursov. Frank made a low whistling sound.

"Wow! I thought my boss had a talent for getting himself into shit, but you top him. The Russian Mafia, eh? They're really nasty boys."

"Tell me about it. What about the disk?"

"C'mon into my lab," Frank said. "I'll see what I can do."

He led me into another room where a scarred wooden desk and worn office chair sat next to a rumpled double bed. The top of the desk was covered with electronic gear, including a personal computer.

"Do you work in your bedroom?" I asked.

"Sure. Some nights, I can't sleep, so I hop on the Internet for a while. Moving my gear in here made everything easier. Let me boot up Old Betsy here and we'll have a look at your disk."

I stood behind Frank as he sat down at his PC. He inserted my DVD into the drive and muttered under his breath as he worked. A few minutes later, he turned to face me.

"Good news, Matt. Your boy only did a quick delete."

"What does that mean in English?"

"The deletion program didn't overwrite any of the data. It just flagged all the files as deleted in the DVD's file index, so their space could be reused. I've got a utility program that can rebuild the index."

"Will we be able to read the files?"

"Probably."

"Do it."

"Okey Dokes. This may take a little while, though."

"Go ahead," I said. "I've got the time."

Fifteen minutes later, we were able to read the contents of the DVD and I understood why Yuri Kursov didn't want the police to find the data. Eric Weisman had kept details about each transaction, including when he'd received the payment, from whom, the dollar amount and where he'd invested the money. Eric's journal could provide the cops with enough evidence of money laundering and tax evasion to have Kursov tending his butterfly collection in prison for a long time.

"This is great, Frank," I said. "Please make a copy of the disk for me. I can't afford to lose this information, whatever happens."

"Sure."

Frank burned a DVD and held it out to me.

"Thanks a million," I said. "You've literally saved my life. I'm going to put the copy into a safe place. Some goons have tossed my apartment already and I'm pretty sure they were looking for this disk. If somebody does get the original, I'll still have the copy as an ace in the hole."

"Why don't you go into a safer line of work, Matt? Like disarming land mines or something."

"I guess I just enjoy pain. Anyway, you're a prince for helping me out, Frank. Can I buy you lunch to show my gratitude?"

Frank grinned.

"Twist my arm. I was going to just warm up some of this pizza, but I can't pass up an offer like that."

"Good. Is there a restaurant around here that you like?"

"There's a great Greek place just down the street. You should try their calamari. It's out of this world."

"Sorry, but I'm not a calamari person. Maybe they can whip up a souvlaki or something for me. Let's go there."

"I gotta warn you, Matt. It's not the cheapest place in the world."

"The sky's the limit. I'll even spring for some garlic bread."

"Wow!" Frank said. "Girls must love a big spender like you. Let me get my coat."

TWENTY-SEVEN

When I got back to the office, Samantha saw me walk in and flashed a Cheshire cat grin.

"Matt, I think I found out something about your boy Raintree."

"Well, don't keep me in suspense. What is it?"

"I did some Net searches about Shawncrest Academy, but all I found was advertising and routine PR stuff. After that, I went downtown to the Toronto Reference Library and scanned through the digital editions in their newspaper morgue. I looked for any stories about Shawncrest from around twenty years back. Here's what I found."

She handed me a print out of a newspaper story with the headline "Shawncrest Schoolboy Goes Missing". Thirteen year old Donald Prescott missed bed check at his dormitory on June 17, 1976. At first, the school staff thought Donald had simply gone home without telling anyone. When his parents reported they hadn't seen him, the police were called in. At the time the article was written, Donald had been missing for three days and the police had just announced that they suspected foul play.

"There were a few follow up stories," Samantha said. "Nothing new in any of them. Eventually, the whole thing got moved from the front page to back with the grocery ads before the media lost interest entirely. So far as I know, the boy was never found."

"Thanks, Sam. This is good stuff. You're definitely not just another pretty face."

"Not an ugly one either, I hope. Do you think this has anything to do with why Raintree is all twisted up?"

"I don't know. Were there any other incidents or scandals at Shawncrest?"

"None that I could find."

"Then it's a good bet that Raintree was involved in the Prescott boy's disappearance or knows what happened to the kid. It's just too big a coincidence otherwise."

"Are you going to follow up on the story?" Samantha asked.

"I was hired to locate David Raintree, that's all. This article is interesting because it may explain what's driving the guy. The Prescott boy's disappearance itself isn't my case. Tonight, I'll meet with whoever shoved that note under our door. Maybe he knows where David is."

"I still don't think you should go to that factory, Matt. It smells like a trap."

"Don't worry, Sam. I'll be careful. You and I were supposed to go out to dinner. Got any specific place in mind.?"

"I know I said I wanted to go to a restaurant, Matt. Would you mind terribly if we went back to my place instead? I'll fix you a home cooked meal."

"You've talked me into it."

"Great. Can you give me a ride? My car is in the shop for some brake work, so I had to take the bus to work. You know how traffic is at this time of day. If we leave now, we'll just manage to pick Tess up from school and we can all go home from there."

"Fine, Sam. I'll just get my coat."

As we drove south on Don Mills Road, we passed Fairview Mall. I noticed an electric sign over the shopping center's main entrance that was displaying a video clip of Santa Claus cavorting in his flying sleigh. That reminded me of something.

"Sam, have you done your Christmas shopping yet?"

"Most of it. I'm trying to keep things simple this year. Why?"

"What have you bought for Tess? I'd like to get her something."

"That's sweet, Matt, but you don't have to do that."

"I'd like to anyway."

"All right, but I'll go with you to pick out her gift. No more earrings. Understand?"

"Yes, Ma'am."

Samantha gave me directions to Theresa's school, a single story brick building located on a tree lined side street. As we drove up, kids were streaming out from class. Toting their heavy book bags on their backs, they looked like slaves bringing loads of ore up from a mine. Samantha spotted Theresa in the crowd and opened the car door to call to her. Theresa ran up to my Toyota, pulled open the right rear door and climbed in.

"Hi, Matt," she said. "I've got something for you."

Theresa took a large brown envelope out of her book bag and held it out to me. Inside were five color photographs of Theresa, dressed in her ballet tutu and striking various poses.

"Thanks, Tess," I said. "You make a beautiful looking dancer."

"I know. It's what I want to do when I get big."

"You'll have to get those arithmetic marks up first," Samantha said.

Theresa gave me a look that said she knew I understood, even if her mother didn't.

I had no desire to get caught in a crossfire between Theresa and Samantha, so I said nothing. I started the car's engine and checked the mirrors for traffic before I drove back out into the street. While we rode along, Theresa told me more about her dancing. I tried to pay attention, but heard about one word out of every five.

When we reached Samantha's house, Theresa took her books upstairs. About five minutes later, she came down again with a mint green gym bag.

"I'm ready, Mommy," she said. "I packed my pajamas, my toothbrush and everything."

"Is Tess going somewhere?" I asked.

"Just next door," Samantha said. "Her friend Cindy is having a pajama party and sleepover for some of the neighborhood girls."

"Can I go now, Mommy?"

"Yes, Honey. If anything happens, call me on your cellphone."

"Oh, Mommy! It's just next door. Nothing will happen."

"Fine, but just call if anything does. Now, run along."

Theresa came over and gave me a hug.

"See you later, Matt. Are you going to come and see me dance next time."

"Wouldn't miss it. Have a good time at Cindy's"

"I will. She's going to have scary videos."

Theresa took her gym bag and ran to the front door. A minute later, I heard the door slam and I turned to face Samantha.

"Well, it's just you and me, Kid," I said. "Want some help in getting dinner together?"

Samantha walked over and put her arms around me.

"Matt, we're all alone and you don't have to go to your meeting for at least three hours. I thought we could do something more fun than dinner and eat later."

"I might disappoint you. I'm still sore from that beating."

Samantha kissed me on the mouth and whispered into my ear.

"Just do the best you can, Darling."

I did.

TWENTY-EIGHT

Around nine o'clock, I drove slowly past the Aurora Mills garment factory with my car's lights switched off. The mystery man's note had specified I meet him there at ten o'clock. Just in case he was planning an ugly welcome for me, I wanted to be there before he got things set up.

The Aurora factory was a single level brick building with a small concrete office complex tacked onto the front. The main building looked as plain as a slab of cheese, but the office area had been designed in that dumbed down Art Deco look that was popular during the early 1960s. A small parking lot sat out front for staff and visitors, with a larger loading yard in the back. From the road, I couldn't see any lights on inside the office building.

As I circled the block, the halogen street lamps along Ellesmere Road lit things up well enough for me to make out three vehicles parked near the factory. All of them were lined up at the curb across the street. A black Ford SUV sat behind a battered green pickup truck and a small gray Japanese sedan. I'd no way to tell whether any of them belonged to the guy I was supposed to meet.

I parked my Toyota about half a block away from the other vehicles and left the car's doors unlocked, in case I needed to make a hasty departure. As I crossed Ellesmere, I decided not to go in through the factory's front entrance. If somebody was waiting in ambush, that would be what he'd expect. Instead, I headed down the driveway that ran along the side of the building. I kept walking until I reached the loading yard at the back.

I don't mind admitting that I was nervous. Anybody who meets strangers at night in deserted factories has to be very stupid not to feel some apprehension.

When I reached the loading yard, I saw two huge metal sliding doors that controlled access to the factory from the concrete cargo dock. Those doors probably weighed tons and needed electricity or hydraulics to operate them. I wasn't going to get in that way. Farther along the back wall of the factory building, I found something better.

A small guard shack had been grafted onto the main building and the shack was secured by a metal door with only a standard key lock. Fortunately, there was no guard on duty. I reached into my overcoat and pulled out a small green canvas tool roll I'd brought with me. The picks and other tools inside were a gift from a friend who'd retired from a very successful career as a burglar. Along with the tools, he'd given me a few lessons.

The lock was a regular dead bolt type and not that hard to pick, if you knew what to do. After a couple of failed attempts, I felt the bolt move and heard the lock click open. I pulled on the door and stepped inside. A second door separated the guard shack from the main factory building, but that door wasn't locked. I was in.

The interior of the factory was totally dark. I pulled a stainess steel penlight from my coat and cupped my hand over the glass as I switched it on. I'd have to be careful because the light could make me an illuminated target. I heard nothing, so I took a chance and swept the beam of the penlight around the room.

Huge rolls of cloth and skeins of yarn had been piled high along the wall on my left, while a line of bulky machines sat in the center of the floor. Along the base of the right hand wall, a row of tables waited with scissors and other cutting tools lying on them. The air inside the place reeked of fabrics, chemical dyes and solvents.

Now that I had some idea about where it was safe to walk, I switched the penlight off and put it away. I took the Glock out of my coat and held it, with the muzzle down, in a two handed firing grip. As I moved slowly through the darkness toward the office complex at the front of the factory, my breathing was shallow with tension. There was still complete silence. A second later, a light came on in one of the offices that were just ahead of me.

I pressed myself against the side of one of the machines and listened. I heard no movement. The person who'd switched that light on might be unaware I was around or he might be waiting for me to show myself. I listened some more. Nothing.

Slowly, I moved toward the lighted office, trying not to make any noise. I was only a short distance away and standing close to one of the concrete columns supporting the factory's roof, when I realized I'd stepped into the pool of light. Something hit the column next to me like a hammer blow and flying chips of concrete stung the side of my face. A split second later, I heard the sound of a gunshot.

I dove for the floor and rolled back into the protection of the darkness as two more bullets whizzed after me. One chewed into the floor near my leg and the second slug smacked the steel body of one of the machines before it whined away in a ricochet.

I crawled a little farther into the darkness, stopped and listened again. My heart was beating so loudly that I thought my attacker would hear it.

The shooter switched the light off again and everything was back in darkness. He'd used that light to draw me out where I could be seen. I'd been the moth circling a flame. My attacker had an advantage because he'd seen me, while I had no idea where he was hiding. I needed to change that.

My right foot brushed something that was lying on the floor and I reached out to pick the object up. It was a cold, smooth cylinder of metal that I recognized, even in the dark. Some factory worker had tossed his empty soft drink can onto the cement floor. The can gave me an idea.

I rolled onto my belly, propped myself up on my elbows and lobbed the empty pop can high and to my left. Somewhere off in the darkness, the can landed with a clatter. I was using the oldest trick in the book, but my assailant went for the bait. He fired twice toward the sound of the can and I saw the muzzle flashes from his gun. Now, I had a rough idea of where he was.

I pretended I was at the practice range and aimed my Glock before I squeezed off a three shot pattern toward the flashes, putting one bullet slightly to the left, one in the center and one to the right. As soon as I stopped firing, I rolled again so I wouldn't be targetted based on my own gun's muzzle flashes. If nothing else, I'd sent a message to the shooter that I was armed and ready to fight back.

I stayed prone on the floor while I waited for return fire, but none came. My ears were still ringing from the shots I'd fired and my mouth was dry with tension. Don't let anybody tell you there's anything cool about a gunfight. Bullets do obscene things to flesh and bone.

A door slammed somewhere in the office area, but I didn't move right away. I'd been tricked into showing myself once already and I didn't want to repeat the mistake. Finally, after what must have been twenty more minutes, I stood up before I switched on my penlight and moved carefully toward the front of the factory. So far, I seemed to be alone.

When I reached the place where I'd seen the gun flashes, I swept my penlight's beam around the area. Three ragged holes in one wall showed where the bullets from my gun had gone in. I saw something else too. Spots of blood on the floor. Not much, but enough to prove I'd made a lucky hit on my assailant. I'd wounded the guy just badly enough to make him lose interest in playing cowboys and indians.

I walked into the front office area where I found the door to the street unlocked. As I stepped outside, the cold night air hit me like a slap in the face. Across the road, the battered pickup truck and the Japanese sedan sat where I'd seen them earlier. The black SUV was gone. I cursed myself for not taking down the SUV's license number when I'd first seen it, but the vehicle hadn't seemed important at the time.

The final score was that I had a scratch on my left cheek from flying concrete fragments, I'd come within a whisker of being riddled with bullets and I didn't know one new thing about David Raintree's whereabouts. It had been just another successful evening in the life of Matt Ryan Super Detective.

What I did know was that I was getting too close to finding out something, so the mystery shooter wanted to stop me permanently. If only I knew what that something was.

When I got back to my car, I took out my cellphone and checked my voice messages. There were two from Laura and she sounded upset. When I called her number, she answered immediately.

"You promised I'd see you tonight, Matt."

"Sorry, but something came up. I'll there in half an hour."

"Please hurry. I really need you."

"I'm on my way," I said and switched off the phone.

As I shifted my Toyota into gear, I realized I was setting myself up for more trouble by spending time with Laura. Sooner or later, Samantha was going to find out. Unfortunately, I'd promised Laura I'd come over and I have a habit of keeping my promises. It's a weakness I haven't overcome yet.

TWENTY-NINE

When I walked into the lobby of Laura's apartment building, Jack Hornsby wasn't at the security desk. Maybe he'd managed to get a night off for a change. Jack had been replaced by an acne faced kid who thought he ruled the universe. I guess I was in a bad mood because of the kind of night I'd been having, but I wasn't amused by the young guy's superior manner. He seemed to enjoy demanding photo ID and making me sign the visitors book. It took a serious effort to restrain my urge to massage the punk's forehead with the butt of my Glock.

Finally, the kid called Laura to confirm that she expected me. Satisfied at last, he pressed the button that unlocked the doors to the elevator area.

"You can go in now," he said with a smirk.

"Thanks," I said. "I'll tell the folks at <u>Stasi</u> Headquarters you're doing a fine job."

I left him staring after me as I went inside and stepped into one of the elevators. When Laura opened the door to her apartment, she looked tired. She was wearing a burgundy bathrobe over cyan silk pajamas. She certainly had a fascinating way of filling out pajamas.

"I thought you'd never come," she said.

"Are you all right?"

"No, I'm not. As well as seeing my patients, I've spent all day with making arrangements for Larry's funeral. I haven't taken any pills either. It's been absolute Hell."

"Withdrawal symptoms. I know about those."

"It's more than that, Matt."

We both sat down on her black and white sofa.

"First Eric was murdered and now Larry," Laura said. "Where does it end? I thought I knew where my life was going. Now, I don't..."

She started to cry. I moved closer to put my arms around her.

"We can't bring Eric or Larry back," I said, "but you're still here. They'd both want you to move on with your life."

I knew I was spouting bromides, but had no idea what else to say.

"You must think I'm such a wimp, Matt."

"You don't need to apologize for having feelings."

"Will you come to Larry's funeral? His parents died years ago and I'm afraid I may be the only one there."

"I'll come if you like," I said.

"Thank you, Darling. I've needed to talk to you so badly all evening. Where have you been?"

Briefly, I told her about what had happened at the garment factory. She pulled away and stared at me.

"My God, Matt! You could've been killed."

"That was the general idea."

"And your face. I should've noticed that cut before."

"Just a scratch. One Band-Aid will make me good as new."

Suddenly, I began to shiver and couldn't stop.

"What's wrong?" Laura asked.

"Sorry. It's just stress, I guess. I've been beaten up and shot at this week. Everything's catching up with me."

"Wait here," Laura said and left the room.

Still shaking, I stood up and walked to a window. I opened the slats of the Venetian blind and looked down at University Avenue. A glowing river of car headlights flowed by as traffic moved through the city streets below. Down there, people lived ordinary lives, worrying about mortgages or griping about unreasonable bosses. At that moment, I envied them.

Laura came back into the room, carrying a paper drinking cup. She held out her left hand and I saw a small white pill sitting on her palm.

"Take this. It will help."

"Thanks, Laura. I know you mean well, but..."

"Take it. It's just a mild sedative. I know what I'm doing, Matt. I'm a doctor. Remember?"

I swallowed the pill with some water from the paper cup. The sedative dissolved before I swallowed it, leaving a bitter tang in my mouth. Laura pulled an adhesive bandage from a pocket of her robe, unwrapped it and stretched it over the cut on my left cheek.

"We make a fine pair," I said. "You're trying to get off drugs and I'm taking more of them all the time. Let's talk for a while. Tell me why you decided to become a doctor."

We sat down on the couch again.

"I had no choice," Laura said.

"What do you mean?"

"Daddy just assumed Eric would follow in his footsteps and become a surgeon. It nearly killed him when my brother dropped out of medical school. I couldn't hurt my father like that again, so I became the doctor instead."

"But not a surgeon."

"I don't have Daddy's surgical skill. Being a GP was the best I could manage."

"Was your father pleased?"

"Not really. For him, surgery was the only real medical discipline. Besides, in Jewish families, it's 'my son the doctor' not 'my daughter the doctor'. Nothing I did ever really pleased Daddy. I wasn't Eric, you see."

"You can stop trying to please your father, Laura. He's dead, so he won't care."

"I just wanted him to love me, Matt."

Laura started to cry again and I took her back into my arms.

"I envy you," Laura said after a moment.

"Why?"

"Because you have a job where you deal in justice."

"If I ever trip over justice, I hope I'll recognize it. All I deal with are people who are cheating and hurting each other."

"Then why do you do it?"

"Now and then, I actually help somebody. That lets me kid myself that I'm making a difference. It's not much, but it keeps me going. Let's change the subject. Why did Eric go to Shawncrest Academy?"

"Daddy thought it was the best school of its kind," Laura said. "If my father hadn't been such a famous surgeon, Eric would never have been accepted. Those rich *goyim* will never admit it, but they don't like their children to rub shoulders with Jews."

"Did Eric ever mention a boy named Donald Prescott?" I asked.

"Prescott? I don't remember that name. Why?"

"The Prescott boy went missing while Eric, Larry and David were at Shawncrest. I think his disappearance was connected to whatever it was that bothered the three of them."

"You must be mistaken. Eric would never have gotten mixed up in anything like that."

"Maybe he wasn't directly involved, but I think he knew what happened."

"Do you think the Prescott boy's disappearance had anything to do with Eric and Larry being killed?"

"I think it had everything to do with their deaths, but I don't know why yet."

"That word 'hangman' written in blood. What does that mean?"

"I don't know," I said. "I think David wrote that word onto the wall at Eric's place and we know he sprayed it onto Larry's car. I think somebody else left it at Larry's house."

"Why somebody else?"

"When David wrote the word, he scrawled it out both times in a loopy longhand. The person who killed Larry printed it in block letters. Larry's killer wants us to think that David shot Larry."

Laura was silent for a minute before she turned to look at me.

"Matt, I'm not going to be able to kick these drugs. I feel awful and don't even know how I'll sleep tonight."

"Stop trying to quit cold turkey. It's all right if you taper off gradually. Just don't lie to yourself about how many pills you're taking. I know it's hard, but you can do it."

For a moment, we sat in silence before I stood up.

"I'd better go home," I said. "I could really use some sleep. That sedative you gave me is starting to work."

"You can sleep here tonight, Matt. You let me stay at your place."

"Yeah and I felt like a zombie after sleeping on that sofa bed. Tonight, I need my own mattress under me."

Laura stood up and walked to the door with me. As I was pulling my overcoat on, she reached out and stroked my face.

"I don't know why I'm so crazy about you," she said. "You're not even good looking."

"Ouch!"

"You know what I mean, Matt. You're no pretty boy. I thought you were a tough guy, but now I see you have a sensitive side too. I guess I just feel safe with you. I know I can trust you completely."

"Never trust anybody completely. Not even yourself."

"I'll bet you trust that girlfriend of yours."

"Her name's Samantha. Yes, I trust her pretty well. I should introduce you to her sometime. You'll like her."

"No, I won't. I'll hate her because she has you."

"You're just a little strung out. Take a pill and get some sleep. You'll feel better in the morning."

"Will I see you tomorrow?"

"I have a lot to get through tomorrow, but I'll phone you in the evening to find out how you're doing. You've taken a big step by starting to get off the drugs, Laura. Just hang in there and I promise things will get better."

"Good night, Darling," Laura said.

Before I realized what she was doing, she leaned forward and pressed her mouth against mine in a long, lingering kiss. I have to admit I didn't fight hard to get free. Just for a moment, going home didn't seem like a such good idea.

"Good night," I said and opened the door to the hallway. I wanted to get out of there before I did something I'd regret later. When I reached the lobby, the young guard was still at his desk. He scowled at me.

"I didn't like that crack you made earlier," he said.

"*Pogue ma hon*," I told him with a smile.

"What?"

"That means 'I apologize' in Irish," I said.

"All right then. Just watch it from now on."

Walking out of the building, I smiled as I wondered how long it would be before the kid found out what that Gaelic expression really meant.

THIRTY

Next morning, Samantha was busy with some filing when I walked into the office. It didn't take a long time for her to notice the adhesive bandage on my face.

"What happened to you?" she asked.

"I got hit by some flying chips of concrete."

Briefly, I told her about the previous night, leaving out my visit to Laura. Samantha turned pale.

"Thank heavens you're all right," she said. "Have you been to the police?"

"I'm going to call Sergeant Beck in a few minutes."

"No wonder people say those Russian gangsters are ruthless."

"It wasn't the Russians, Sam. The guy who shot at me probably killed Eric Weisman and Larry Holt. He's worried that I'm going to find out something. I just wish I knew what it was."

"Do you need anything, Matt?"

"No, thanks. I'm fine. Anything urgent in the mail?"

"Just the usual bills."

"I'll look at them later. Right now, I need to make some phone calls."

I walked to my desk and sat down in my swivel chair before I picked up the telephone. After I switched my computer on, I watched it boot up while I called Beck's number.

"Toronto Police Service. Sergeant Beck speaking."

"It's Matt Ryan. I thought you'd like to know that somebody tried to kill me last night."

"Really? Can't say I'm surprised. What happened?"

"I got an anonymous note from somebody claiming he knew where to find David Raintree. I was supposed to meet him last night at the Aurora Garment Factory, out on Ellesmere Road. When I got there, the guy started shooting. I fired back and I think I hit him before he took off."

"How do you know that?" Beck asked.

"He left some blood behind. Not a lot, so I don't think I did much more than scratch him. It probably won't help to check the hospitals."

"You should've let me assign a couple of men to watch your back, like I offered. Much as you bug me sometimes, Ryan, I'd hate to find you in an alley. Did you get a look at the shooter?"

"No. Everything happened too fast. I know he drives a black Ford SUV, but that doesn't narrow things down much."

"You were bullshit lucky to hit anything at all in the dark," Beck said. "Found out anything new about Raintree?"

"No. What about you?"

"We're still looking for him. He's smart. I have to give him that. He hasn't used his credit cards or tried to contact his mother. The twerp knows how to fly under the radar. By the way, you're not keeping me in the loop, Ryan. You didn't tell me Raintree dyed his hair."

"Like you forgot to tell me about the Seabreeze Motel?"

"Okay, Ryan. We both have to do better at keeping each other informed. Anything else?"

"Not for now."

"Fine. Keep me posted. Sure you don't want a bodyguard?"

"I'm sure. Thanks anyway."

"It's your funeral. Bye, Sweetheart."

I heard a click followed by the dial tone.

"Thanks for your concern," I muttered to myself.

Something bothered me about my conversation with Beck, but I couldn't think what it was. Finally, I shrugged and called the next number on my mental list. Rebecca Raintree picked up after three rings.

"It's Matt Ryan," I told her.

"At last! Have you finally found my son?"

"No. I'm calling to apologize about that. I feel like I've failed you, Mrs. Raintree, so I won't take any more of your money. I'll keep looking for David anyway. I don't like to give up on a case."

"David's been gone three weeks now, Mr. Ryan. I'm so worried about him that I don't know what to do."

"I'm sure he's still alive, Mrs. Raintree. He's just trying hard not to be found."

"For Heaven's sake, why?"

"I wish I knew. Did he ever say anything to you about a boy named Donald Prescott he knew at Shawncrest Accademy?"

"Prescott? Not that I remember. Why?"

"The Prescott boy went missing while David was at Shawncrest. I think his disappearance has something to do with David's strange behavior."

"David would never get mixed up in anything like that. By the way, I've just found out something that worries me. David has a gun with him."

"What? How do you know that?"

"After the war, my father brought back a German officer's pistol as a souvenir. I kept it in a locked case in the library. Because I rarely look at it, I noticed it missing only yesterday. David knew where I kept the key to that case. He must have taken it."

"Thanks for letting me know, Mrs. Raintree."

"Will that gun get my David into any trouble?"

"I hope not. Try not to worry. If I find out anything new, I'll let you know. Goodbye for now."

"Goodbye, Mr. Ryan."

After Mrs. Raintree hung up, I let my breath out in a long sigh. Now, I was looking for a deranged man with a gun. This was turning out to be a swell week.

My third phone call was going to be the tricky one. I pulled the drawer of my desk open and took out the note I'd received from Yuri Kursov. Near the bottom of the page, below the picture of a blue butterfly, there was a phone number. I called that number and listened to a phone ring five times on the other end of the line.

"*Da?*" asked a voice that sounded like it was coming from a gravel pit. I guessed I was talking to Stone Face, Kursov's hulking bodyguard.

"Let me talk to Mr. Kursov."

"You have wrong number."

I lost whatever dregs of patience I had left.

"Look," I said. "I have something Mr. Kursov wants. If you don't get him on the phone, he won't get it. If that happens, your life won't be worth a piece of used toilet paper. Tell him Matt Ryan is calling. Right now."

For a moment, there was dead silence at the other end of the connection. I imagined the expression on the giant's face as he thought about what he wanted to do to me for talking to him like that.

"You wait," he said.

The next voice I heard was Kursov's.

"Mr. Ryan. How good to hear from you. I was becoming worried because your time is almost up. For your sake, I hope you have good news for me."

"I have your ledger, Kursov. It's on a computer DVD."

"Excellent. I will send one of my men for it."

"Not a good idea. This is very sensitive information. I want to give it to you personally."

"You are right, of course. Where shall we meet?"

"I'll be in front of First Canadian Place at noon," I said. "The Adelaide Street entrance."

"I shall be there. Until then, Mr. Ryan."

I heard a click as Kursov hung up.

"What was that all about?" Samantha asked. She'd heard only my end of the conversation.

"I'm meeting the Russian mob boss at noon."

"Are you crazy, Matt? He'll kill you."

"I don't think so. I'll be giving him what he wants. Just in case I'm wrong, you'll find a DVD in the drawer of my desk. It's a copy of the files I'm giving to the Russian. Very incriminating stuff. If I do get killed, give that DVD to the police. I'll have the satisfaction of taking Kursov down with me at least."

"Your satisfaction? What about mine? What do I do if they kill you?"

"Sorry, Sam. My job has its risks."

"Your job is for lunatics, you mean. How often are you going to risk your life like this?"

"As many times as it takes. I've go to face up to dealing with the Russians. They'll only come after me if I try to run from them."

I picked up Kursov's copy of the DVD, found my coat and started for the door. If I drove to the subway right away, I'd get downtown with a few minutes to spare. When I tried to kiss Samantha goodbye, she turned her face away at first before she threw her arms around me.

"Come back safe, Darling."

"I'll try, Sam. It's up to Kursov."

As I headed for the parking lot, I didn't feel nearly as brave as I pretended.

THIRTY-ONE

A perpetual wind blows through the concrete canyons of Toronto's downtown core. All of those tall buildings distort the natural air flow and the heat escaping from tens of thousands of offices creates weird micropatterns of weather. As I stood in front of First Canadian Place, sleet stung my face the air felt ten or fifteen degrees colder than the official temperature. Despite my parka, gloves and watch cap, I was starting to feel numb.

Farther down Adelaide Street toward Bay, a man in a Santa Claus suit stood minding a glass charity donations kettle. Santa was stamping his feet to keep them from freezing and booming a mirthless "Ho, ho, ho" at everyone who passed. Seeing him made me feel better. Finally, I'd found a guy who had a job even worse than mine.

A black Mercedes sedan with tinted windows pulled out of the passing traffic and glided to a silent stop at the curb near me. The right rear window of the sedan whined down and I saw Yuri Kursov's face smiling at me.

"*Dobri den*, Mr. Ryan. You look cold. Get in. We will take a ride."

I walked around the back end of the Mercedes and opened the left rear door. As I climbed in opposite Kursov, I saw a dark haired guy in a leather coat who was riding up front with the driver. He was pointing a silencer equipped pistol at my chest. Kursov noticed my reaction and smiled.

"Do not let Serge worry you. He is always ready to protect me. You are looking well, Mr. Ryan."

"For somebody just out of hospital, I'm doing all right."

"I must apologize for that. My men were not told to beat you so badly. Unfortunately, I have idiots working for me. Did they cut your face too?"

"No, that was somebody else. A lot of people want to rearrange my appearance these days."

"How unfortunate," Kursov said. "Perhaps we should talk about business now. You told me you have my files."

"They're on a DVD in my coat. If I reach for it, will Serge give me a few new buttonholes with that pistol of his?"

Kursov laughed and spoke to Serge in Russian.

"Just move slowly, Mr. Ryan, and all will be well," he said.

I pulled the DVD out of my parka pocket and gave it to Kursov.

"How do I know these are the right files?" he asked.

"When you see the contents, you'll know."

"Then you have looked at the files?"

"I had to look at them to be sure I had the right disk."

Kursov nodded.

"How can I be sure there are no copies?"

"You can't be sure, but I doubt it. Weisman's sister told me Eric had only one disk. He wouldn't let anyone see it, not even her."

"And you believe her?"

"Yes, I do. Weisman and Holt were the only ones involved with you in the money laundering. They're both dead, so you have no worries."

"Larry Holt is dead?"

"Somebody shot him yesterday. I don't think it had anything to do with these files. He and Weisman were involved in some mess that happened when they were in school together. It seems to have come back on them."

Kursov looked at me carefully.

"What about you, Mr. Ryan? Have you made copies?"

I thought about the DVD sitting in my office drawer and hoped that Kursov couldn't read my mind.

"I've got no use for the information unless I wanted to blackmail you, Kursov. I'm not that stupid."

Kursov seemed satisfied. He shoved the DVD into a pocket of his expensive overcoat and pulled out a thick manilla envelope.

"You have done well, Mr. Ryan. Here is your reward."

"Thanks, but I don't want your money," I said. "I'd prefer something else."

Kursov's eyebrows went up slightly in surprise.

"And what might that be?"

"You're a powerful man, Kursov. Some day, I may be in trouble and need a favor. I ask only that you remember I did you a service."

Kursov nodded and I could tell that he felt flattered.

"I will remember. You are unusual, Mr. Ryan. I am beginning to like you. Would you be willing to work for me?"

"You could never trust me."

"Why not? Are you not an honest man?"

"That's exactly the problem."

"You sound like my Uncle Leonid," Kursov said. "He was a true *vor*, a professional criminal. He survived even Stalin. When I was a boy, he told me to never trust an honest man. He said that, when you need such a man to do something for you, he will always suffer an attack of ethics."

"Your uncle was very wise."

"Yes, I think so. You have given me a pleasant day, Mr. Ryan. I wish you the same. You will notice we are back at the same spot where we picked you up. *Do svidaniya*."

I knew I was being dismissed, so I opened the car door and stepped back out into the cold. As I left the Mercedes, I looked back and saw a sad look on Serge's face. I think he was disappointed that I'd given him no reason to shoot me.

The black Mercedes glided back into the traffic, leaving me standing alone on the sidewalk. Down the street, Santa was still suffering his chilly misery. To escape the bitter wind, I took refuge in the warmth of First Canadian Place and headed back to the subway.

As I moved past the upscale stores in the underground shopping mall, I felt as though a load had been lifted from my shoulders. Maybe I'd shaken off the Russian bear. Only time would tell for sure.

When I got back to the office, Samantha was still out for lunch. A moment after I sat down at my desk, the phone rang.

"Matt? It's Frank from *The Parkdale Drop In Center*."

"Hi, Frank," I said. "What's up?"

"Are you still looking for that guy Raintree?"

"Absolutely. Have you heard anything?"

"Better than that. He's here right now."

"Are you sure?"

"Positive."

"Keep him there. I'm coming right over."

"The guy's acting weird, Matt. I don't know if I can hold him."

"Nail his shoes to the floor if you have to. I'm on my way."

I hung up the phone, grabbed my parka and headed for the door.

THIRTY-TWO

Despite dry roads, it took me nearly forty minutes of fighting traffic to get out to Parkdale. This time, I wasn't lucky enough to find a parking spot right out in front of the *Parkdale Drop In Center*. I had to circle the block twice before I saw somewhere to leave my car. As soon as I'd parked, I ran back to the Center's green front door.

The air inside was as stale and rank with tobacco smoke as I remembered it. Four haggard looking men sat in a cirle in the front room while they played cards. They didn't even look up when I walked in.

"Where's Frank?" I asked.

One of the card players turned his head to stare at me with bloodshot eyes.

"Back in the dining room with the weird guy," he said.

"Gin," said the man next to him. I didn't know whether he was referring to his hand of cards or to his favorite beverage.

I walked down the narrow hallway toward the kitchen area and found the dining room on my left. Through the open doorway, I saw Frank.sitting at a long table that was covered by a cheap plastic table cloth imprinted with images of poinsettias. David Raintree sat across from him.

Raintree was barely recognizable. His hair was a tangled mix of blond and black after the amateurish dye job he'd done on himself. He still wore a dark blue business suit, but it was wrinkled and stained after he'd lived in it for weeks. His gaunt face bristled with an unkempt beard and his eyes were red from lack of sleep. A steaming bowl of Frank's beef stew sat in front of him on the table.

"Here's Matt Ryan now," Frank said as I walked in.

Raintree looked up at me with suspicion.

"Are you a cop?" he asked.

"Private investigator. Your mother hired me."

"Mother hired you? Why?"

"To find you. She's worried about you, especially now that your friends Weisman and Holt are both dead."

Raintree's eyes widened in surprise.

"Larry's dead? How?"

"You didn't know? Someone shot him and used his blood to write the word 'hangman' on the wall. Sound familiar?"

Raintree reacted as though I'd jabbed him with a cattle prod. He jumped to his feet, upsetting his chair and sending the bowl of Frank's stew spilling onto the linoleum floor. As Raintree turned toward the doorway, Frank reached across the table and grabbed at his sleeve.

"Wait," Frank said. "You don't need to be afraid."

"Let go of me," Raintree shouted. He pulled away from Frank's grasp, reached into the right pocket of his suit jacket and pulled out a Luger P08 pistol. It was a sixty-five year old antique, but still deadly.

"Easy, David," I said. "You don't need the gun."

"Mother didn't send you, Ryan. You're really working for him."

"Who?" I asked.

Raintree didn't answer. Instead, he moved toward the door and I saw Frank getting up out of his chair.

"Don't," I said to Frank, but it was too late.

As Frank lunged toward him, Raintree turned and fired his Luger. Frank's feet went out from under him and he hit the floor hard. I pulled my Glock out of my parka, but Raintree was out of the room already and running down the hallway toward the street door. Instead of chasing him, I knelt beside Frank. His eyes were open and he was struggling to sit up.

"Don't try to move, Frank. I'll call an ambulance. Where did he hit you?"

Frank looked up at me as though I was an idiot.

"Damn it, Matt, he missed me. I slipped on some of that stew he spilled on the floor."

For a moment, Frank and I looked at each other before we both burst out laughing. Frank winced when he tried to stand up.

"I sure landed hard, though," he said. "I'll be black and blue for days."

"Trying to tackle Raintree was stupid. You could've been killed."

"You saw him, Matt. The guy's a ticking timebomb and he has a gun. Somebody better stop him before he goes on a shooting spree."

"He's started one already, with you. It's just a good thing he's a lousy shot."

Leaving Frank to fend for himself, I went out into the hallway. The door to the street was ajar, allowing gusts of icy wind into the building. I walked out onto the front sidewalk, but there was no sign of Raintree. As I went back inside, I put my gun away and took out my cellphone. Sergeant Beck was his usual charming self when he answered.

"You again? What is it this time?"

"I'm at the Parkdale Drop In Center, Beck. David Raintree was just here. He has a gun. An old German Luger. He took a shot at the guy who runs this place, but he missed."

"Is Raintree still around? I'll come right over."

"No. He took off. I don't know where he is now."

"Just what this town needs, Ryan. Another nut bar with a gun."

I thought about reminding Beck that I was a "nut bar" myself, but decided against it.

"I just thought I'd give you a heads up, Beck."

"I appreciate that. Don't worry. We'll be careful with Raintree when we find him."

"If you find him," I said under my breath. "Well, it's been lovely to chat with you, Beck, but I have to go. *Do svidaniya.*"

"Who?"

"Just a little Russian expression I picked up. Bye."

I switched my cellphone off and put it back into my coat. Raintree's reaction when I told him Larry Holt was dead convinced me that he hadn't been involved. I doubted he'd killed Eric Weisman either. Raintree seemed to be afraid of a mysterious someone who was driving this whole mess. Could that mystery man be Yuri Kursov? If I could find out who was pulling the strings, things might start making sense.

THIRTY-THREE

When I returned to where I'd left my Toyota, I saw a dark blue Ford sedan parked behind my car. Two men got out of the vehicle as I pulled out my car keys. Both guys were Caucasian, had dark hair and wore black overcoats. The younger one was taller than his partner and both men's faces had the impassive expression favored by cops and gangsters. I wondered what kind of trouble I was in this time.

"Hold on there a minute, Ryan," the taller man said.

I turned to face the two as they walked up to me.

"Do I know you?" I asked.

"We know you, Ryan," the shorter guy said.

"Is that right?"

I slid my right hand into the coat pocket where I carried the Glock.

"Keep your hands where we can see them," the taller man said.

"Easy, Bob," said his partner and he smiled at me, displaying tobacco stained teeth. I tensed when the shorter guy reached into his own coat, but he pulled out a billfold instead of a gun. He flipped it open so that I got a glimpse of an identity card. It showed his photo, a picture of a bison head and the motto <u>Maintiens</u> <u>Le</u> <u>Droit</u>. My two pals were Mounties.

"We just want to talk," the shorter Mountie said. "It's too fucking cold out here. Let's sit in our car."

He held open the front passenger's door of the blue Ford and I climbed in. Bob got into the back of the car while his partner slid in behind the steering wheel.

"What does The RCMP want with me?" I asked.

"You have the wrong friends," Bob said from the back seat.

"Let me handle this," said the shorter man.

Bob scowled, but he nodded. It was obvious who was in charge.

"Sure, Jimmy," Bob said.

"Know a man named Yuri Kursov?" Jimmy asked me.

"We've met."

"What's the nature of your business with Kursov?"

"I don't have any business with him."

"You've been seen with him, Ryan."

"If you're tracking Kursov, then you know he's a loan shark. I'm working a missing persons case. I went to see a man named Eric Weisman because I thought he might know something. When I found Weisman, somebody had blown his head off with a shotgun. Weisman owed a lot of money to Kursov. I guess Kursov thought I might have found some of it at Weisman's place. He was wrong."

I didn't mention Eric's files. I'd heard a lot about the Mounties and not all of it was good. I wasn't sure I trusted these guys much more than I did Kursov.

"Is that why Kursov put you into the hospital?" Jimmy asked.

"You boys have done your homework."

"We've been watching you for a while, Ryan. I can tell you what you had for breakfast."

"All right. Kursov was hard to convince, but he knows by now that I don't have anything of his. I don't expect to see him again."

"That's where you're wrong," Bob said.

"I said I'd handle this," Jimmy said. "Ryan, we want you to contact Kursov and offer to work for him."

"Why would I do that?"

"So you can learn about his operations and report back to us."

"You want me to be your snitch."

"Think of it as helping law enforcement. You want to help your community, don't you?"

"Sure. That's why I buy Girl Guide cookies every year."

"Maybe you think this is funny, Ryan, but we're not laughing. Loan sharking is one of Kursov's more benevolent activities. If there's any form of organized crime he hasn't gotten into, it's only because he hasn't found the time yet."

"I'm sure he's careful not to get his own hands dirty," I said.

"You got that right. We've been working with CSIS on Kursov for more than a year. So far, we'd have a hard time nailing him for illegal parking. That's why we need your help" "

"And if I refuse?"

"That would be a mistake," Jimmy said. "We'd be forced to go over your detective business with a microscope. Everybody has got something to hide. For example, you seem to have a habit of stumbling over dead bodies."

"Are you threatening me?"

"I'm just telling you how things are, Ryan. These are troubled times. With everybody so scared of terrorism, law enforcement agencies don't have to use kid gloves anymore. If we found anything on you at all, you'd lose your license. If you were really dirty, then who knows what might happen?"

I realized I was being forced to pick which horse to back, either Kursov or Jimmy. I decided on Kursov. At least the Russian gangster didn't hide behind the law when he threatened me.

"Sorry," I said. "You'll have to find somebody else."

"Don't flatter yourself, Ryan," Bob said from the back seat. "We don't need you that bad. We have a mole inside Kursov's organization already."

"Any other secrets you want to tell him?" Jimmy asked as he turned to glare at his partner.

"I'm leaving now," I said to Jimmy. "Have a nice day. Next time, I hope they assign you a partner with a brain."

I got out of the Ford and walked to my own car. The two Mounties sat there and watched as I drove away. I couldn't decide whether Bob's remark about having an informer in Kursov's gang had been a genuine slip or just a clever ruse. Maybe the Mounties wanted to see what I'd do with a tidbit of information. Would I try to sell it to Kursov?

When I got back to my office, I took the DVD containing copies of Eric Weisman's files out of my desk and slipped it into my coat. When I got home, I'd cut the disk into pieces and put it into the trash. I'd kept the files as a little bargaining chip, in case Kursov thought about killing me. Now, the information was too dangerous. If the Mounties hadn't searched my office already, they would very soon. If they found so much as a gum wrapper that I couldn't explain, they'd use it against me. Bugging the premises would be standard too. From now on, I'd have to be careful about what I said, whether using the phone or not.

Samantha walked in, wearing her coat and carrying a box of printer paper.

"I had to pick up some supplies, Matt. Can we leave now? I need to get Tess a little early today."

"I got a scratch on my car this afternoon, Sam. Come outside with me. I want your opinion about whether I should bother getting it painted."

Samantha started to say something, but I put my finger to my lips and she took the hint. We walked out into the parking lot and stood next to my Toyota.

"What's going on, Matt?"

"From now on, assume that our office is bugged. I got picked up by two Mounties today. They want me to spy on Yuri Kursov for them and I refused. They'll be looking for anything they can get to put pressure on me."

"Matt, this just keeps getting worse. First the Russian Mafia, now the RCMP. Where does it all end?"

I looked at Samantha and realized I didn't know the answer.

THIRTY-FOUR

Smantha had invited me to dinner at her home, so we drove together to Theresa's school. A warmer air mass had moved into the city during the afternoon and most of the remaining snow cover had melted, leaving brown lawns and an illusion of Spring. Samantha and I met Theresa before we rode out to Downsview, fighting rush hour traffic all the way.

After we reached the house, I was watching TV with Theresa when Samantha came out of the kitchen.

"Tess, I'm out of bread," she said. "Would you and Matt please go to the shopping center and buy two loaves? You know the kind we usually get. Here's a ten dollar bill."

"Can't I go later, Mommy? Opra is on now."

"We need the bread for dinner, Honey."

"We can record Opra and watch her later," I said to Theresa. "It's a nice mild evening, so we can walk over to the center. It'll be fun."

"All right," Theresa said reluctantly. With an ease that surprised me, she used the remote to program the DVD recorder before we went to the hall closet to get our coats.

After we'd left the house, Theresa looked up at me solemnly.

"Mommy can be a real pain sometimes," she said.

"Some day, you won't think she's so bad."

It was just turning dark and many people still walked along the sidewalks, on their way home from work. We turned off Bathurst before we crossed the street and headed toward the small shopping center that Samantha had mentioned. Theresa was a few steps ahead of me when she stopped suddenly and looked back.

"Are you and Mommy going to get married?" she asked.

I was caught completely off guard.

"I don't know, Tess. We haven't talked about anything like that."

Theresa put her hands on her hips and looked at me.

"You'll never be my Daddy," she said.

"I know your father was a great guy, Tess. I can never replace him and I don't want to try. Whatever your mother and I decide, I just hope you and I can still be friends. Okay?"

Theresa weighed my answer for a moment before she smiled.

"Sure. I guess that would be all right. Can I look at the toys while we're at the shopping center?"

"All right, but don't tell your mother."

"It'll be our secret," Theresa said.

We bought two loaves of whole wheat bread and Theresa ogled the toys in a discount department store before we headed back toward home. As we walked up Theresa's street, there was no motor traffic except for a black SUV that was moving toward us, on our side of the road. I couldn't see the SUV well in the dark, but it looked like the same vehicle I'd noticed that night at the garment factory. I grabbed Theresa around the waist and threw us both flat on the ground, just as the black Ford sped by us. I heard two loud bangs and gouts of dirt flew up close to my face.

The Ford's tires squealed as it lurched to a stop and began to turn around. The driver was coming back to finish the job. By now, I'd pulled my pistol out of my overcoat. I got up on one knee, gripping my gun in both hands, and took aim at the black vehicle roaring toward me. The glare of its headlights blinded me, but I aimed at where I hoped the driver was sitting and squeezed off two rounds. I thought I saw one bullet spider web the windshield glass, but I couldn't be sure.

I threw myself flat again as the SUV roared by, but there was no return fire. A second later, the Ford was gone and everything was quiet again. On the ground near me, Theresa was crying. When I scooped her up in my arms, she seemed to be unhurt.

"Are you all right?" I asked.

"I'm so scared, Matt. Why were you shooting?"

"I had to do it. Somebody in that black car was trying to hurt us, but it's all right now. He's gone and you're safe."

"No, I'm not. I skinned my knee when you pushed me down."

I kept my arm around Theresa while we walked the rest of the way home. She seemed to be badly shaken up and I wasn't much better off. What I really dreaded was telling Samantha.

"My God!" Samantha said when she heard what had happened. "This is too much, Matt. If you and I are in danger, that's one thing. Having someone shoot at Tess is another."

"I know. Maybe you and Tess should go away for a few days, just until things cool off."

"I can't pull Tess out of school right now. She's in the middle of Christmas term exams."

"Then stay away from the office for a while. Whoever shot at us tonight was after me, not Tess. You both ought to be safe, so long as you're not near me."

"I don't want to be away from you, Matt. I love you."

"It's just for a few days. It won't be easy for me either, but I don't want to put you and Tess in danger on my account."

Samantha looked at me for a moment and then she nodded.

"All right. Just for a few days. Promise?"

I took Samantha into my arms and kissed her.

"I'm going to clear up this case as soon as I can, Sam."

"It can't be soon enough, Darling. I'm going to be worried sick about you."

"Don't be. I have nine lives like a cat."

Theresa walked in from the kitchen, apparently recovered from her fright.

"Mommy, I'm hungry," she said.

"All right, Honey. Let's have dinner before the chicken gets cold."

THIRTY-FIVE

Next morning, I made sure that I left Toronto early because I had nearly a five hour drive ahead of me. Aylmer is a small town near Ottawa that has a growing Mennonite community and is known mainly for the production of wine, canned fruit and jams. It's also the home of The Shawncrest Accademy For Boys.

As I sped east on Highway 401, the city skyscrapers thinned out to be replaced by factories and shopping malls. Eventually, they all disappeared too and I was moving past small dairy farms. It was a bitterly cold day, but I was grateful for sunny breaks and only a few light snow flurries. Even when I was much younger, I disliked long drives. Now, I dread them.

Many people are sentimental about small towns and rural areas, but I'm not one of them. Homes out there are isolated and any law enforcement is thinly spread. Country people don't pry into their neighbors' activities for fear of being shunned as meddlers. Everybody in small communities works hard to appear bland and inoffensive. When I look at some wholesome farm family, I wonder whether they go home to have sex with the livestock or to practice cannibalism. I admit that cities have their share of crime and violence. For real depravity, you have to go out into the country.

About half way to Aylmer, I stopped at a highway service center so that I could use the bathroom and have lunch. The food prices in the restaurant area would have made Jesse James blush. After chewing my way through a cardboard sandwich and drinking a cup of watery coffee, I was on my way again. I didn't stop again until I was at the outskirts of Aylmer, where I filled the Toyota's gas tank and asked for directions to Shawncrest Accademy.

The school looked very much the way I'd imagined it. Gray stone Victorian buildings sat on sprawling campus grounds that were partially surrounded by a stone wall. The large wrought iron gates were open, so I drove up the long gravel driveway and parked my Toyota outside what seemed to be the main building. A gust of icy wind hit me as I stepped out of my car, so I wasted no time going inside.

The vestibule had a black slate floor and large stained glass windows. For a moment, I thought I was in Westminster Abbey. A white haired man wearing steel rimmed glasses sat behind an oak desk located to the left of the entrance. He was shivering in his thin shirt, so I pulled the heavy front door closed behind me to shut out that killer wind.

"May I help you, Sir?" the white haired man asked.

"I'm Robert Fisk. Dean Peters is expecting me."

I handed him a phony business card I'd brought with me.

"Very good, Sir. Will you wait here a moment, please?"

The old man stood up and left the room through a door at the back of the vestibule. While I waited, I studied the stained glass windows. The images depicted in them were confusing, but it all seemed to be about a war between dragons and serpents. I was beginning to cheer for the serpents when the old man returned with a younger man who had dark curly hair.

I guess I'd expected Dean Peters to be smoking a pipe and wearing a tweed jacket with leather elbow patches. This younger guy didn't look more than thirty-five and he wore an open necked pink shirt under a loose fitting gray silk suit. Academia was changing.

"Good afternoon," he said as we shook hands.

"Dean Peters?"

"I'm Harvey Ellis, the Registrar. Dean Peters was called away suddenly on an urgent metter. He apologizes and has asked me to help you."

"Fine," I said.

Ellis turned to the white haired man.

"That will be all, Ronald. I'll call you if we need anything."

Ronald went back to his desk while Ellis pointed me to the door through which he'd come into the vestibule.

"Let's go back to my office."

We went through the doorway and down a hall to a large room that had a great view of the grounds. I pulled up a chair as Ellis settled himself behind his large desk. Ellis steepled his hands and looked at me.

"Your business card says you're a lawyer, Mr. Fisk. How can I help you?"

"I have a client looking for a good school for his son and he learned about Shawncrest from one of your alumni."

"Well, we're always grateful for good references."

"That's just the thing, Mr. Ellis. My client has heard Shawncrest is an excellent school, but he's concerned about something that happened here. One of your students disappeared and was never found."

"You must be referring to the Prescott boy's disappearance. That happened twenty years ago."

"Nevertheless, he sent me to ask about it, just to assure himself his son will be safe here."

"The Prescott thing was before my time, Mr. Fisk. I've only been here for about eight years now. I do know no blame was assigned to the school. It was just one of those tragic incidents that could've happened anywhere."

"Why weren't the police contacted until after the boy was missing for forty-eight hours?"

"As I told you, I wasn't working here then. I've only been told a little about what happened. Prescott had run away from school once before. Because there was no evidence of foul play, the faculty naturally assumed he'd done it again. His parents were away for the weekend and couldn't be contacted immediately. As soon as they reported their son hadn't come home, we notified the police."

"Were any of the other students questioned?" I asked.

"Of course. They all were. None of them knew anything."

"Three of the students knew the Prescott boy very well. Their names were Raintree, Weisman and Holt. Was there any suspicion that they were involved?"

"I wouldn't know, Mr. Fisk. I wasn't here. We keep all student records confidential, so I wouldn't tell you anyway. You seem very well informed. Are you sure you're just checking for a client?"

I realized I was blowing my cover.

"I'm just repeating what I've heard," I said. "One more thing. I understand your school plans some renovations to the grounds."

"That's right. We plan to begin as soon as Spring arrives."

"What have you got scheduled?"

"How is that relevant to your client?"

"Anything I can learn about Shawncrest will give him a better picture," I said.

"Very well. We plan to do some landscaping, reopen the old well and do repairs to a number of the buildings. Nothing dramatic. Just some maintenance that's long overdue."

I decided I wasn't going to learn anything else, so I stood up.

"Thanks for your time, Mr. Ellis. I'll tell my client I was very impressed by Shawncrest."

"Thank you. Please do that."

Ellis watched me with suspicious eyes as I left his office. It would be dark within two hours and I didn't relish the five hour drive back to Toronto, so I went into town instead. I wound up checking in at The Pinecrest Motel. After eating a surprisingly good stir fry at a Chinese place across the road, I went back to my motel unit and stretched out on the bed. An old Elvis Presley movie flickered silently on the room's TV set as I thought about the Raintree case.

I couldn't help being disappointed about obtaining so little new information after coming all the way from Toronto, but I hadn't expected much. The Shawncrest faculty wanted to treat Prescott's disappearance as ancient history, so that the whole thing would be forgotten. They were succeeding.

I couldn't shake the notion that whatever happened to Donald Prescott was connected to David Raintree's erratic behavior, but I was no closer to proving it.

Either I was more tired than I realized or else the Chinese cook had slipped a little something extra into my stir fry. Before I knew it, I'd drifted off to sleep. I dreamed I was chasing Raintree through a swamp. The closer I came to catching up with him, the higher the dark water rose around me. Just as I reached out to grab David, I slipped and sank deep into the foul smelling ooze.

I woke up sweating and checked my wristwatch to learn it was still only ten o'clock. On a cold night in a town like Aylmer, there was nothing for me to do but watch more bad TV for a while before I tried to sleep again. This time, I managed it without the bad dreams.

THIRTY-SIX

When I got back to Toronto on the next day, it was about three o'clock in the afternoon. I took a quick shower before I sat down at my chess board to finish my end game against Capablanca. Despite being dead, he was winning. Of course, Capablanca was supposed to win because I was playing a classic game out of a book. Still, I hate losing. I decided to quit chess for a while and listen to some Irish music.

As beautiful as I think Irish music is, I know it sounds strange to anyone who doesn't have Celtic ancestry. I was losing myself to the rhythm of *bodhrans* and *uilleann* pipes when my phone rang. It was Laura and she sounded frantic.

"Matt, can you come over right away?"

"What's wrong?"

"Someone broke into my apartment while I was at the clinic."

"What? Is he still there? Get out and call the police."

"Don't worry. Whoever it was, he was gone when I came home. I don't want to deal with the police right now. They'll ask too many questions and my head is spinning as it is. My place is a total mess. Can you come over?"

"I'm on my way."

After I left my apartment and locked the hallway door, I stretched a small piece of transparent tape across the seam between the door and the frame. If anybody broke in while I was away, I'd find the tape had been disturbed. It's a cheesy old trick, but it still works.

When I reached Laura's apartment building, Jack Hornsby was working the security desk again.

"Afternoon, Shamus," he said. "I see nobody's killed you yet."

"You won't believe how many people are trying, Jack. Did you make everybody sign in today?"

"Sure. I always do, but I just came on duty an hour ago. The new kid should be working this shift, but he called me at home. Said he was having stomach pains and asked me to cover for him. So, here I am. Why are you asking about my signing people in?"

"Somebody broke into Dr. Laura Weisman's apartment today."

"Shit! Well, he didn't get past me. Between you, me and the bedpost, the new kid is useless. He'd let a biker gang ride through the lobby without raising a peep."

I remembered the young guard being rigorous enough with me, but I didn't want to argue with Hornsby.

"May I see the visitors register?" I asked.

"Sure."

Hornsby turned the registry book around, so that I could read the pages. I didn't really expect to find any useful information. Any burglar with half a brain would have used an alias.

"Maybe the perp didn't come in through the lobby," Hornsby said. "He might've sneaked in through the parking garage, just like the nut who spray painted that car. You can get right onto the elevators from the garage."

"Haven't you beefed up garage security yet?" I asked.

"Nope. I'm still fighting with building management about that. It's like arguing with a turnip."

"Thanks, Jack. I'm going up to see Dr. Weisman now. Can we talk again later?"

"I'll be here. You've been seeing a lot of that lady lately. You're a lucky guy. She's a real looker."

"We're just friends, Jack."

"Right. And I'm Winston Churchill."

When I pushed the doorbel button at Laura's apartment, she didn't open up right away.

"Who is it?" she called out.

"It's Matt."

When Laura opened the door, I saw that she was trembling.

"I'm so sorry to bother you again, Matt, but I didn't know who else to call."

"It's all right. Show me the damage."

Laura led me through her apartment, so I could see that drawers had been opened and papers scattered on the floor. Over all, the intruder had left less of a mess than the two Russians dolts who'd tossed my place, but I didn't think Laura would find that news comforting.

"Everything was like this when I came home, Matt."

"Is anything missing? Cash or jewelry?"

"No. Nothing like that."

"Then this was no robbery. The burglar was searching for something specific."

I went back to check the hallway door. Laura's place was on the nineteenth floor, so no burglar would come in through a window. Whether the perp had scammed his way past the security desk or sneaked in through the garage, he would've entered through that hallway door. The lock showed no sign of forced entry. We were dealing with a pro.

"Matt, does this have anything to do with Eric's files?"

"I doubt it. Kursov wanted those files and I gave them to him. He'd have no reason to send somebody to search your apartment."

"You don't know what a shock it was for me to find this."

"It's a good thing you weren't here, Laura. The intruder probably didn't plan to hurt you, but he might have panicked if you'd surprised him. Anyway, it's all over now. I'll help you tidy up."

"I can't sleep here tonight, Matt. Somebody has been here, pawing through my lingerie. I feel violated."

"I can understand that. All right. Let's put things back together. You can stay my place for a day or two, until you feel better."

"Thank you, Darling. I really appreciate that."

I helped Laura tidy up a little and she packed a small suitcase before we went down to the lobby. Jack Hornsby looked up from reading his newspaper as we approached the security desk.

"Sorry about the break in, Dr. Weisman," he said. "Have you called the cops?"

"No. Nothing was taken. I'm tired this evening and I don't want to answer a lot of police questions."

"Sure. Sometime in the next couple of days, I'll have to ask you to fill out an occurrence report though. Sorry, but building management makes me do that whenever a break in happens."

"Of course, Jack. You can give me the form next time I see you."

Hornsby turned to me with a grin on his face.

"Maybe Dr. Weisman should hire you to solve this one, Shamus."

"No thanks, Jack," I said. "I've already got a case that's driving me crazy. It involves a couple of murders and a boy who disappeared from Shawncrest Academy, about twenty years ago."

"Shawncrest Academy? You mean that school for rich kids in Aylmer?"

"That's the one," I said.

"You wouldn't be talking about the Prescott boy, would you?"

"Jack, that happened twenty years ago. How can you possibly remember?"

"Because we never solved it. It's the unsolved cases that keep you up nights. I was with the Ottawa force back in those days. Ottawa is a government town, so it's pretty quiet compared to Toronto. We didn't get many missing persons investigations."

"Did you work the Prescott case personally?"

"Not me, but we all knew about it down at the station. The boy's disappearance was a big story for quite a while, his parents being rich and all. If you want details, ask your pal Beck."

"Sergeant Joe Beck?"

"Well, he wasn't a sergeant in those days. Just an ambitious young bastard who'd just been promoted to detective. Beck was all over that case like a heavy sweat. I was real surprised when he didn't crack it. After a while, we all moved on to other things."

"Thanks, Jack. You don't know what a help you've been."

"Don't mention it. An old copper like me doesn't get many chances to be useful."

We left Laura's Volvo at her apartment building and used my Toyota to drive to my place. A misty drizzle was falling, making the city streets look mysterious and slightly romantic. As we walked into the lobby of my apartment building, I noticed that the super had put holly wreaths up on the walls. I'm not a Christmas type of guy, but I liked the effect. Laura and I took the elevator up to my apartment. When I checked the door, the tape I'd left seemed to be undisturbed.

While Laura unpacked, I heated up a couple of frozen dinners and tossed a salad. After we ate, we talked while we listened to jazz on my old stereo. Laura sat close to me on my sofa, leaning her head on my shoulder. Finally, I looked at my watch.

"I'd better get out the spare sheets," I said. "Looks like I'm going to spend another night riding the sofa."

Laura put her arms around me and gave me a look that elevated my blood pressure.

"Don't be silly, Matt. Your bed is big enough for both of us."

"We've been through this before."

"Have we?"

Before I could answer, she pressed her mouth against mine. I don't know how long the kiss went on, but I was hoping it would last all night. Finally, we came up for air.

"I've told you I'm in a relationship," I said. "If something did happen between us tonight, it would be just a one time thing."

"Fair enough. I'll take anything I can get, Darling."

I could offer excuses about how beautiful and seductive Laura looked or blame her perfume. None of that would be the truth. I knew exactly what I was doing.

"All right," I said. "You can stop chasing me because you've caught me. For tonight at least."

Laura smiled and began unbuttoning my shirt.

"It's about time," she said.

THIRTY-SEVEN

Early next morning, I drove Laura downtown to her apartment building. From there, she could collect her Volvo and drive it to her medical practice. She kissed me on my cheek before she got out of my Toyota.

"Last night was wonderful, Matt. See you this evening."

Standing on the sidewalk, Laura waved as I steered my Toyota back into the traffic and headed north.

We hadn't bothered breakfast before we left my place, so I stopped at a Tim Horton's for two muffins and a cup of hot tea. Back at my office, I sat at my desk and sipped the tea while I chewed away at the muffins. I barely tasted them. The food was fine, but my appetite had been deadened by guilt.

I knew I'd betrayed Samantha's trust on the previous night, so I was glad she was staying away from the office. I couldn't face her without having her sense my infidelity. What made matters worse was how good sex had been with Laura. Much to my surprise, we'd been like old lovers. I felt ashamed, yet a part of my mind couldn't wait to be with Laura again. Somehow, I had to concentrate on work and forget her for a while.

I picked up my phone and called Sergeant Beck's number.

"Toronto Police Service. Sergeant Beck speaking."

"We need to talk, Beck."

"Oh, it's you, Ryan. Okay, go ahead and talk."

"I mean face to face."

"Sounds serious. Do you know Fran's Restaurant on College Street? It's just off Yonge."

"I know the place, but why don't I just come down to the station?"

"I'd rather keep this just between us, Ryan. I'll be in Fran's at noon. Come hungry. They've got a great blue plate special."

Beck hung up before I could say anything else. I puttered around the office for a couple of hours as I realized how much I depended on Samantha to keep the place going. Around eleven, I got my parka and walked out to the parking lot. After I left my Toyota at the Don Mills subway station, I rode the southbound train to Wellesley, came back up to street level and walked down The Yonge Street Strip.

"The Strip" is a ten block slice of the surreal. Stores selling bibles sit next to strip clubs, S&M clothing shops and places that peddle hassish bongs. Upscale fashion stores nestle next to walk up porn shops where lonely men masturbate to movies in back rooms. If you've got the street price and the right contacts, you can buy anything on The Strip. Whether you want rare comic books, porn, guns, dope or teenage sex slaves, it doesn't matter. Step right up and show us the color of your money.

In the doorway of a store that advertised cheap electronics gear for sale, I saw a gaunt man sitting cross-legged in front of an upturned baseball cap with some coins in it. He wore a badly scuffed brown leather bomber jacket and torn blue jeans that needed to be hosed down. The people passing by ignored him as they concentrated their Christmas giving on relatives and friends who owned too much already. I saw that the guy's face was red with the cold as he looked up at me.

"Got any spare change?" he asked.

I remembered a five dollar bill in my wallet, so I pulled it out and dropped it into the baseball cap. The homeless man grinned as though I'd passed him a winning lottery ticket.

"Jesus! Thanks, Man. Merry Christmas."

"I doubt it," I said, "but I appreciate the thought."

As I reached the corner of College Street, I passed a store window showing a mix of leather bondage gear, porn videos and a collection of hunting knives. One stop shopping for serial killers.

Fran's Restaurant is a Toronto landmark, a last remnant of the small chain of eateries founded in 1940. The place is clean, cheap and features the kind of food my mother would have served, if she'd known how to cook. It was lunch hour, so the place was filled with customers and noisy. The air inside felt as warm and steamy as an orchid house as I stepped in from the bitter cold outside. I had to look around the room for a minute or two before I noticed Beck sitting in a booth near the back. Despite the warmth in the restaurant, he still wore his overcoat.

I threaded my way past the scurrying waitresses until I reached Beck's booth and took off my parka before I slid in across the table from him. He was busy devouring a steak and a mound of fries from a plate in front of him.

"Don't you feel hot with that coat in here?" I asked.

"Nope. I picked up a bitch of a cold somewhere and I can't shake it. I feel chilled all the time."

"Instead of steak, maybe you should've ordered chicken soup."

"You're a million laughs, Ryan. Why are we here?"

"I want to know why you didn't tell me about the Prescott case."

"Who?"

"Come on, Beck. Don't tell me you don't remember young Donald Prescott's disappearance. Jack Hornsby does."

"Really? Well, don't put too much trust in that old fart Hornsby's memory. He was put out to pasture because he could barely remember how to find the men's room. Hornsby was a good cop, once upon a time. Now, I hear he's flying the security desk at some snooty apartment compex. It's sad, actually."

"Don't change the subject, Beck. Why didn't you mention the Prescott boy? Hornsby told me you worked the case."

"Okay, I guess I should have told you about it. It's a case I'm trying to forget, Ryan. I don't like to dwell on the ones I couldn't solve. Some rich kid went missing from a poof school near Ottawa and he was never found. So what? That was twenty years ago. Why is it so important now?"

"Because I'm convinced Prescott's disappearance is connected to the murders of Eric Weisman and Lawrence Holt."

"No shit? How do you figure that?"

A plump waitress came over to take my order, but I waved her away.

"Weisman, Holt and Raintree were all at Shawncrest Academy together," I said. "Weisman's sister told me something happened while they were there that scarred them all emotionally. They'd never talk about it to her. I think that whatever happened was connected to the Prescott boy."

"You're grabbing at straws," Beck said. "As I recall, the Prescott kid wasn't happy at Shawncrest. He ran away from the place once before. I think he tried to hitchhike home and got picked up by some pedophile creep who killed him."

"But no body was ever found."

"We looked. Even had dogs out. There's a lot of land up that way, Ryan. I think Prescott is still buried in some farmer's field."

Beck cut a piece off his steak and chewed it vigorously.

"What about Weisman's murder and Holt's?" I asked.

"At first, I thought Weisman got popped by a burglar. After Holt got snuffed and the word 'hangman' showed up again, I changed my mind. I think your boy Raintree offed them both."

"Why would he do that?"

Beck speared some French fries with his fork.

"Who knows? Raintree's mother admits her son has been a couple of cards short of a full deck for years. Now he's gone completely nutso. Maybe Raintree sees himself as some kind of some kind of divine avenger on a mission from God."

"Maybe, but I still think all this has to do with something that happened at Shawncrest."

"Fine. If you want to spend your life chasing moonbeams, that's your business."

"Your theory doesn't explain one thing, Beck."

"Yeah? What's that?"

"Somebody tried to kill me twice and I'm sure it wasn't David Raintree," I said.

"Twice? You told me about the garment factory. When was the second time?"

"The same guy tried a drive by shooting the other night, while I was walking home with Samantha's daughter Theresa. If this clown wants to get me, that's one thing, but he could have killed a nine year old girl."

"Maybe your shooter has nothing to do with Weisman, Holt or Raintree, Ryan. I'm sure you're working other cases. Maybe you've pissed off somebody connected with one of them. Maybe it's just your friggin' personality. Who knows? Come down to the station and fill out a statement. I can assign somebody to watch your back."

"Twenty-four seven, for the rest of my life? No, thanks."

"Suit yourself. You going to order anything to eat?"

"I'll grab some lunch later. Right now, I have somewhere to go. Thanks for the chat, Beck. Let's stay in touch."

"Just like two peas in a pod," Beck said with his mouth full of fries.

I picked up my parka, stood up and headed for the door to the street. Outside the restaurant, I was still zipping up against the cold when I heard someone tooting a car horn. When I looked up, I groaned to myself. The blue Ford sedan with my buddies Jimmy and Bob inside was parked at the curb.

"Get in," Jimmy said. "This time, we really are going for a ride."

THIRTY-EIGHT

Jimmy and Bob drove me all the way out to Newmarket. I sat in the back of the Ford while Jimmy drove and Bob lounged in the front passenger's seat. Every time I asked why I'd been picked up, Jimmy changed the subject with some small talk about the weather or a sports game. Finally, he told me that all would be revealed after we reached the RCMP field office.

Half an hour later, I sat across a scarred wooden table from Jimmy in a dingy interrogation room. Bob leaned against one wall and chewed gum.

"Want to tell me why I'm here?" I asked.

Jimmy smiled and leaned back in his chair.

"We just want to give you a chance to reconsider your decision to not work with us," he said. "We want to be reasonable about this."

"Otherwise, we'll break your balls," Bob said.

"Spare me the good cop bad cop routine, Fellows. This isn't the first time I've been brought in by the police."

"That's for sure," Jimmy said. "You've got a fascinating rap sheet, Ryan. You started off with a bang by killing some German guy while you were in the army."

"It was the air force and that was an accident."

"Aren't they all? You've come close to having your PI license pulled so many times, we've lost count. You bend the rules until they look like pretzels, Ryan. Lately, you've been found at two murder scenes that we know about. With an exciting life like that, what do you do for relaxation?"

"Farming," I said.

"Farming?"

"Yeah, I sit around and watch cops like you shovel bullshit."

Jimmy sat up straight and glared at me.

155

"I see I'm boring you," he said. "Maybe you'll find this amusing."

He reached into his suit jacket, pulled out a folded sheet of paper and handed it to me. All I saw were paragraphs of legal jargon in dense print. Near the top of the document, I noticed the names "Sergeant James Flynn" and "Corporal Robert Bradley". They had to be my pals Jimmy and Bob.

"What's this?" I asked.

"It's a Crown search warrant. As we speak, a team is removing all records from your office. It's part of our investigation of certain allegations against you. Don't worry. Our guys didn't kick your door down, though that would have been fun. The building manager spoiled everything by giving us a spare key. By the way, your PI license is suspended until further notice."

"This is just harrassment and you know it," I said.

"Cry me a river, Ryan. It doesn't have to go like this, you know. We can make all of this unpleasantness go away. All you have to do is to help us to bring down Kursov."

"Kursov isn't the idiot you think he is, Flynn. He'd see through your scheme in a minute and put a bullet into my head."

"Call me Jimmy. You underestimate your charm, Ryan. We know you've been in Kursov's clutches three times already, yet you're still breathing. That's something of a record. The guy must love you."

"Why do you need me?" I asked. "You guys said you have a mole in Kursov's organization already."

"Did we? You must have misunderstood us. Anyway, we can't have too many moles, can we?"

"Was it your people who ransacked Laura Weisman's apartment?" I asked.

"Ah yes, the lovely Dr. Weisman. You have terrific luck with women, Ryan. You've got that hot looking redheaded secretary and the Weisman babe too. Does either of them know you're banging them both?"

"What about the apartment?" I asked through clenched teeth.

"We don't do illegal searches. Even if we did, you'd never know we'd been there."

Much as I wanted to punch Jimmy's lights out, I believed him about the search. The Mounties probably wouldn't have been so clumsy. Suddenly, I decided I'd had enough.

"Okay," I said. "The party is over. Right now, one of two things is going to happen. Either you're going to arrest me or you're going to drive me home. Which is it?"

Jimmy looked at me for a moment before he shrugged.

"All right, Ryan. You can go. I guess you were joking about our driving you home."

"I wouldn't be out here in Newmarket if you hadn't brought me. How am I supposed to get home?"

"You're the super sleuth. Figure it out."

Cursing under my breath, I left the RCMP detachment and walked along the town's Main Street until I found a banking machine. I withdrew some cash, found a taxi stand and rode southeast to the Don Mills subway station. When I got there, I collected my Toyota from the commuter parking lot and drove out onto Sheppard Avenue.

I'd decided not to go back to my office. If I met any of those Mounties who were carrying my stuff away, I might do something I'd regret later. Instead, I headed for home, feeling lousy. I was going to contact my lawyer, but I knew the RCMP could stall him until Doomsday about getting my records back and having my license restored. In the meantime, I couldn't work as a detective without facing sanctions. Jimmy and Bob had me over a barrel.

When I let myself into my apartment, I was surprised to find Laura there.

THIRTY-NINE

"You're back early," I said.

"So are you, Matt."

"Well, that's because I've had such a swell day."

I told Laura about my meeting with Jimmy and Bob. She looked alarmed.

"How can they ask you to spy on that Russian gangster?" she said. "You might get killed."

"I doubt that idea keeps them awake at night, but don't worry. The Mounties can lean on me, but I'm not going to do what they want. You've heard my sad story. What's yours? Why are you back so early?"

"I've been tapering off on the pills, Matt. Today, I went totally clean. The morning was fine, but I felt awful after lunch. Fortunately, I had fewer patient appointments today than usual. I was able to reschedule everyone and leave the office."

"Good. Let's have an early dinner before you go home."

"I can't go home, Matt. What if that burglar comes back?"

"He won't," I said.

"You don't know that for sure."

I saw that Laura was trembling and realized she was really scared. Still, I knew that I had to get her out of my place if I wanted to untangle my involvement with her. Against my better judgement, I decided to do something.

"There's a little Japanese place just around the corner," I said. "Let's go there for something to eat. After dinner, I'll give you something to make you feel more comfortable."

"Like what?"

"You'll see. Let's go. I'm hungry."

We walked around to the *Takura Bune* and managed to get a table near the main window. Outside, rush hour traffic was clogging up the streets and long shadows were forming in the waning sunlight. As we had our *miso* and *tempura,* I tried to keep the conversation light. I wanted to take Laura's mind off her problems and I didn't want to think about mine.

When we'd finished our meal, I paid the bill and we walked back to where I'd parked the Toyota. As I started the engine, Laura turned to look at me with an expression of curiosity.

"Want to tell me where we're going?" she asked.

"And spoil the surprise? It's just a few minutes from here. Be patient."

We drove east into Scarborough, a huge region of Toronto that has a very mixed character. In the south end, affluent neighborhoods like The Guildwood flaunt expensive homes that have been around for six decades or more. In the north, the Agincourt area has a mushrooming Asian population and is littered with shabby strip malls where guys still sell merchandise out of the backs of trucks. I knew the route we were taking, so I concentrated on checking my car's rearview mirror for evidence that we were being followed. I didn't notice any.

It was already twilight by now and the low cinderblock building I was looking for blended in with the rest of a gray industrial park just off Birchmount Road. A large white sign sign out front read *Safe And Sound Storage – Low Monthly Terms* in black letters. I steered my Toyota into the company's driveway and drove around back where I parked outside Unit 17.

"What's this place?" Laura asked.

"Just a company that rents out storage sheds. I keep stuff here that I use sometimes but don't want found if my office gets searched."

"What kind of stuff?"

"I'll show you."

We got out of the car and I took a key from my pocket to unlock the blue metal door securing Unit 17. I rolled the door up out of the way and we stepped into the dark interior of a storage shed. Inside, the air was as cold as it was outside and the place smelled musty. I found a light switch on the wall and turned it on. The glow from a single electric bulb mounted in the ceiling revealed a row of enameled metal shelves that were stacked with cardboard boxes.

"Welcome to the treasure cave," I said.

From one of the shelves, I pulled down a cardboard box that had a soup company's trademark printed on it. I opened the flaps of the box and showed the contents to Laura. Inside, I'd stored several blue stationery boxes filled with business cards that had been printed with various phony names and company logos.

"I use these when I go undercover," I said.

"What about that crowbar and the other tools over there?" Laura asked.

"Sometimes, I need to get into places by unorthodox methods."

"And you brought me out here just to show me all this?"

"No. I want to give you something. Just a minute."

I put my stash of business cards back into its place and hunted among the shelves for what I wanted. It was a black shoe box that I found on one of the lower shelves. Inside, an object was wrapped tightly in waterproof plastic. I pulled the wrappings away carefully and held the thing up nearer to the light, so I could get a better look at it.

It was a .38 Colt Cobra, carefully cleaned and still smelling of gun oil. Before semiautomatic pistols came into fashion, the Cobra was a favorite weapon for detectives and thugs alike. It was easy to carry, easy to conceal and it fired six slugs that would stop anybody at close range. I broke open the Cobra's cylinder, found some cartridges in the shoe box and loaded all six chambers. When the gun was ready, I held it out to Laura.

"Do you know how to shoot?" I asked.

"I can handle a rifle or a shotgun pretty well. Daddy often took us hunting when Eric and I were little. Handguns aren't my strong suit."

"It's not so different, Laura. Just point and fire. Squeeze the trigger instead of pulling. I got this gun from a client who was a collector. So far as I know, it has never been used in a crime. On the other hand, I don't have a permit for it. I want you to keep it with you for a while for protection. Be careful, though. Don't shoot the poor pizza delivery guy because he knocks on your door by mistake."

Laura smiled.

"I think I can restrain myself. Thanks, Matt. I'll feel a little safer with this."

She put the Colt into her purse and we went back outside. I pulled the storage shed's door down and locked it before we got back into my car. We didn't talk much as I drove to North York. When I pulled into the parking lot of my apartment building, Laura turned to me.

"I guess you want me to collect my things and go home," she said.

"My apartment's too small for two people, Laura. We'll get on each other's nerves in no time. Besides, I think it'll be better if I don't see you for a few days."

"So you can spend time with that redhead?"

"Her name is Samantha. No, I plan stay away from her too. Somebody is working hard to kill me and I don't want to put either of you in danger."

"I'm not afraid as long as I'm with you, Matt."

"Thanks, but you should be. Don't forget that the Mounties are crawling all over me too. Your life will be a lot tidier if we don't see each other for a little while."

"All right, but I have just one question. Do you love me?"

I'd been dreading that question. I looked at Laura and gave it to her straight.

"No, I don't. What scares me is that I could love you, very easily. That would be a terrible mistake. We'd be a disaster as a couple. We're both coping with drugs, for one thing. Besides that, we don't have much in common. A working stiff like me would never fit in with your rich friends."

"That's not fair, Matt. Whatever you want to say about me, I'm no snob."

"I'm sorry. I didn't mean it that way. Let's go inside."

Laura packed the overnight bag she'd brought to my place and then she was gone. I sat at my chessboard and wonderered how to put my life back together. Who was trying to kill me? Why? How could I get the Mounties off my back? Should I have given that gun to Laura? I had lots of questions, but no answers.

When my phone rang, I assumed it was either Laura or Samantha calling. I picked up a white pawn from the chess board with my right hand while I reached for the phone with my left.

"Hello," I said.

"Is this Matt Ryan?"

The room shifted out of focus for a second and the chess pawn dropped from my fingers. I knew that voice.

"David? Is that you?"

"We have to meet," David Raintree said.

FORTY

St. Timothy's Catholic Church is on Leith Hill Road and just a short drive from my apartment building. David Raintree's choice of a church as a meeting place struck me as unusual, but I didn't object. David's dishevelled appearance would attract unwelcome attention in a bar or restaurant and I'd learned to be wary of meeting people in vacant factories.

It was starting to snow when I reached St. Timothy's. The church parking lot was nearly empty, so it seemed no services were scheduled for that evening. I locked my car and zipped up my parka against the cold. Religion no longer means anything to me, but an echo of my Catholic boyhood made me hesitate for a moment about taking a gun into a church. I shrugged the feeling off and kept my right hand on the loaded pistol in my parka pocket. Raintree had a Luger and he'd shot at Frank with it already.

The church was warm inside, dimly lit and nearly deserted. Three old women wearing colored shawls over their heads knelt up front, near the altar railing, as they prayed facing a bank of flickering votive candles. I sat down in one of the rear pews and waited. Several minutes crawled by. Just as I was coming to the conclusion that I'd been duped, I heard someone cough. When I turned my head to the left, I saw David Raintree. He sat a short distance away in my pew and he had his Luger pointed at my chest. I nodded to him.

"Put away the gun, David. You didn't ask me here to kill me."

"I won't shoot unless you make me. Just keep your distance."

"Fine. Why are we here in this church?"

"I like it here. It's so quiet and peaceful. Sometimes, Mother brought me to St. Timothy's when I was a boy."

"I meant why did you want to meet me?"

"You said Mother hired you, Ryan. Why would she do that?"

"I told you before. She's very worried about you."

"Why would she worry about me?"

"Why not? She hasn't seen or heard from you in almost a month and two of your former schoolmates have been brutally murdered."

"I didn't kill Eric and Larry," David said.

"I know you didn't, but you were at Eric's shop the night he died."

"Sure. I went there to talk to him, but he was dead already. The way he looked... I've had nightmares about that ever since."

"Did you write 'hangman' on the wall with Eric's blood?"

"Yes."

"Why?"

"Because I thought Eric's death was his punishment."

"Punishment for what?"

"How did Larry die?" David asked, ignoring my question.

"Shot through the head. Somebody wrote the word 'hangman' on the wall at his place too. I don't think it was you that time."

"No. I didn't even know Larry was dead until you told me."

"What's this all about, David?"

Raintree leaned against the back of the pew. He looked like a very old man who was sagging under the weight of memories he'd carried for too long. His hand trembled as he lowered the barrel of his pistol, but I made no attempt to grab for the gun.

"It was just supposed to be a stupid game," he said.

"It involves the Prescott boy, doesn't it?"

Raintree nodded.

"My God, Ryan! All these years. I need to tell somebody."

"Tell me, David."

"Did you know that Eric, Larry and I went to Shawncrest Academy together?"

"Yes. Eric's sister told me that people called you 'The Three Musketeers'."

For just a moment, David'd face relaxed and he smiled.

"That's right. We did everything together, but we were spoiled and bored. We started tormenting the younger boys for amusement. At first, it was juvenile pranks, like short sheeting their beds or cutting the buttons off ther clothes. Then, things got worse."

"How much worse?" I asked.

"We'd extort money from younger boys and beat them up if they didn't pay."

"Is that what you did to Donald Prescott?"

Even in the dim light, I could see the pain on David's face.

"You know about Donny?"

"I know something happened to him and that you three were involved."

"Donny was one of our favorite targets. He was only thirteen, chubby and wore thick glasses. You know the kind, Ryan. Bright in class but terrible at sports. We made fun of him and did our best to make his life Hell.

One day, Larry said he had a great idea. We'd tell Donny we were forming an exclusive club that only the best people could join. Donny could be a member if he went through a hazing ritual. Of course, there was no club. We'd never let Donny join, even if we had one."

"Did Donny fall for it?"

"Of course. He was so desperate to belong to anything. There was an old shed on the school grounds where the gardener and the maintenance men kept tools and supplies. Larry told Donny to meet us there at ten o'clock one night. The prefects did a nightly bed check on all of us at nine, but they never came back later. It was easy to be there for bed check and sneak out of the dorm afterwards."

"Wasn't that gardening shed kept locked, David?"

"Sure, but the gardener dropped his key ring one day. Eric found it and had the shed key copied at the local hardware store before he returned the ring. After that, we'd use the shed as our private place to go when we wanted to smoke pot or look at porn magazines. We all thought we were pretty cool."

"What happened when Donny showed up?"

"The three of us were waiting for him. We jumped Donny, stripped off his clothes and tied his hands behind his back."

David paused, as though wrestling with what to say next. He looked down at his hands and lowered his voice.

"Eric told Donny he'd have to do whatever we told him if he wanted to pass the hazing. We made him kneel and perform oral sex on each of us."

I just nodded, not thinking David wanted me to comment.

"By now, Donny was crying. He said he didn't want to belong to any club. He just begged us to let him go."

"Did you?"

"No. We knew he'd tell on us and we'd be expelled. Maybe go to jail too for sexual assault. We didn't know what to do. Larry called me to one side and said he had an idea. If we scared Donny badly enough, he might not report us."

"How would you do that?" I asked.

"The maintenance men had left some folding camp chairs and a stepladder against one wall of the shed. Larry found a coil of rope over there too. He climbed the ladder and tied one end of the rope around one of the shed's roof beams. Eric and I opened one of the folding chairs and stood Donny on it. His hands were still tied behind his back, so he couldn't put up much of a struggle. Larry tied the other end of the rope around Donny's neck."

"Donny must have been terrified."

"That was what we wanted. Larry told Donny we were going to play that word game 'Hangman'. Except we were going to play it for real. Donny would have ten chances to guess a word that Larry was thinking about. If he didn't get it right, we'd hang him with the rope."

"What word?"

"There was no word, Ryan. Larry just wanted to torture Donny. Whatever Donny guessed, Larry told him he was wrong. I counted off Donny's guesses until he'd made ten of them."

David paused again. I just waited for him to continue.

"By now, Donny was frantic, just like we'd hoped he'd be. I was supposed to tell Donny we'd forget about hanging him if he'd swear not to tell anybody what we'd done. Before I could say anything, Larry got this weird look on his face, then he kicked the chair out from under Donny. For a minute, Eric and I just stood there gaping before we grabbed the chair and tried to get it back under Donny's feet. It was too late. Donny's neck had been broken by the drop and he was dead."

"What happened then?" I asked.

"Eric and I were furious with Larry, but he told us it was too late to be sissies. We had to get rid of Donny's body."

"How did you do that?"

"Eric remembered an old well that was on the grounds. It had provided drinking water before the school got hooked up to the town water mains. The maintenence men had nailed a board cover over the well mouth, so nobody would fall in. We got a crowbar and hammer from the shed, went to the well and pried the cover off. Larry and I carried Donny's body out to the well, while Eric brought along Donny's clothes. I was so scared that somebody would catch us, but nobody was around at that time of night. We pushed Donny into the well, threw his clothes down after him and nailed the cover back on."

David stop talking as he broke into sobs. I reached out toward him, but he jerked back and pointed the muzzle of the Luger at my chest again.

"Stay back, Ryan."

"Calm down, David. What you three did was terrible, but you were just teenage boys then. Why did you send those notes to Eric and Larry?"

"I read a newspaper story about some landscaping changes at Shawncrest. One of the things they planned to do was to reopen the old well. I knew they'd find Donny's bones, so I wanted Eric and Larry to come forward with me and admit what we'd done. It wouldn't be the first time we'd been found out."

"Not the first time? What do you mean?"

"We all thought we'd been so clever in covering up Donny's death, but he guessed what happened right away. I went into hiding after he killed Eric because I knew he'd want to kill me too."

"Who are you talking about?" I asked.

David shook himself like a dog shedding water and looked at me with weary, red-rimmed eyes.

"Eric and Larry are the lucky ones, Ryan. It's over for them. I'm just so goddamn tired of running and being scared."

He put the muzzle of the Luger under his chin.

"David!" I shouted. "Don't...!"

Before I could move, he squeezed the trigger. I closed my eyes and tried not to retch as echos of the gunshot reverberated through the interior of the church.

FORTY-ONE

The interrogation room at Toronto Police Service's 32 Division will never win any prizes for decor. I sat on a wobbly wooden chair behind a table scarred by cigarette burns and stared at the room's drab gray walls without really seeing them. By now, it was ten o'clock on a night that seemed to have no end. Watching David Raintree end his miserable life in such a gory way had been the last straw. I felt exhausted and burned out. Even the bupropion in my bloodstream couldn't prevent the iron shroud of depression from settling over me again.

I thought about Donald Prescott spending twenty lonely years in his deep grave after three school boys let their boredom drive them to murder. Evil had spilled out of that well to consume Raintree, Weisman and Holt. All three were dead now, but only one of them by suicide. There was still another killer prowling around out there and I was his next target.

The door opened and a cop walked into the room. He was the same stubby detective who'd confronted me at Larry Holt's house.

"Hello, Ryan," he said. "We meet again."

"Do you work out of this division?" I asked.

"No. When I heard you'd been busted, I just had to come down and pay my respects."

"To gloat, you mean."

"Don't be like that, Ryan. You're a fascinating guy. You turn up at all the murders. I wonder why that is."

"David Raintree wasn't murdered. He killed himself."

"So you say."

"There were three old women in the church. Ask them."

"We did. Three old Latvian ladies who were lost in prayer. You and Raintree could've been having an orgy at the back of the church and they wouldn't have noticed. They didn't even see you until after they heard a shot."

"Fine. Check Raintree's gun. You'll find only his fingerprints on it, not mine."

"We're doing that. It might take a few days though. Our forensics boys are backlogged. Meantime, you'll have a nice comfortable cell."

"This stinks," I said. "You know I didn't kill Raintree. You're just throwing your weight around."

"We should have sad violin music for this part, Ryan. I told you I knew how to deal with smartasses like you."

I heard a knock at the door and a blond policewoman came into the room.

"Phone call for you in my office, Detective Smalls," she said.

Smalls grunted and stood up.

"We're not through yet," he said to me and left the room to follow the female cop.

I sat there, too numb to move. So, my runty tormentor was named Smalls. Normally, I'd have a good laugh about that. At that moment, nothing seemed funny.

Two minutes later, Smalls was back and he didn't look happy.

"Get out of here," he said. "Go home."

"Pardon?"

"You heard me."

"Why the sudden change of heart, Smalls?"

"Things have changed, that's all. Now, get lost."

As I walked toward the station's main entrance, I saw the blond policewoman sitting behind a desk in her small office off the main corridor. She was sorting through a pile of papers. I knocked on the door frame and went in.

"Excuse me, Constable," I said. "Who made that call to Detective Smalls just now?"

"That's none of your business."

"It wasn't Sergeant Joe Beck by any chance?"

"I told you. That's confidential information. Get out of my office."

I looked down at the pile of papers on her desk. On top was a memo titled *Protocols For Cooperation With The Royal Canadian Mounted Police.*

"Thanks," I said. "Sorry to be a nuisance, but could I get a ride back to where I left my car?"

The blond constable looked at me as though I'd crawled out from under a toilet, but she picked up her phone.

"Wait out in the hall. I'll check whether any patrol cars are in the area."

I was lucky and two uniformed officers drove me back to St. Timothy's so that I could collect my Toyota. Enough snow had fallen to make the streets slick, so I had to concentrate on my driving as I went home and had no chance of thinking about much else.

When I was safely back in my apartment, I sat on my sofa and turned the details of the Raintree case around in my mind for what seemed like the millionth time. Suddenly, it all clicked into place. If I was right, then Laura was in a lot of danger.

I found my cellphone and called Laura's number. After three rings, her voice mail message came on. Maybe Laura was just out somewhere or maybe something was wrong. I felt my stomach turn over. Instead of leaving a message, I grabbed my coat and gun before heading for the door. My hand was on the doorknob when the phone rang.

FORTY-TWO

"Hello," I said after I picked up the phone receiver.

"I'm surprised to catch you awake, Ryan. It's nearly midnight. I figured you'd be in bed with your teddy bear by now."

"I don't have time to talk to you, Flynn. I'm on my way out."

"Call me Jimmy. I just wondered if you've changed your mind about helping us against Kursov."

"Not a chance."

"Show some gratitude, Ryan. Why do you think the Toronto cops let you walk tonight?"

"I know you leaned on them. Why?"

"I think that's obvious. You can't help us against Kursov while your sitting in a jail cell, now can you?"

"I'm not going to help you, Flynn. Get over it. Why would Kursov hire me anyway?"

"You're a detective. Some say you're a pretty good one. Kursov has people he needs to keep an eye on. You could offer to watch them and report back to him."

"So he can kill them if he doesn't like what I find?"

"Anything you tell Kursov, you'll tell us too. We'll keep the situation under control. What do you say?"

"Guess which part of my anatomy you can kiss," I said.

"You really are a mule headed son of a bitch, aren't you? I'm Irish too, so I can't help admiring that. Still, a smart man knows when he has to bend over. Do you think this is as bad as it gets? We've just started to squeeze you."

"It's been great talking to you, Flynn. I have to go."

I pressed down on the phone cradle to disconnect the call and then decided to try Laura's number again. I was relieved when she answered. Her voice sounded tired.

"What is it, Matt?"

"May I come over to see you?"

"It's late. I was just about to go to bed."

"This is important, Laura. You may be in danger. I can't say too much over the phone because this line is probably bugged."

"Bugged? By whom?"

"The Mounties. The Russian Mafia. Take your pick."

"How soon can you be here? I really am very tired."

"I'm on my way. Bye."

I locked my apartment and headed for the parking lot. When I stepped outside, I cursed to myself. A freezing rain was turning the sidewalks and roads into a skating rink. Rather than driving, I'd get to Laura's place faster by walking to the subway station and riding the train downtown.

As I shuffled along the icy street, trying not to slip and fall, I was angry with myself for not figuring things out sooner. The killer had been two jumps ahead of me all along. I hoped he wouldn't get to Laura before I did.

When I reached Don Mills Station, I caught the first westbound train to the Yonge Street transfer point. The other subway passengers were the usual late night crowd. Bleary eyed shift workers rode home rubbing elbows with buzzed out party animals who'd spilled out of the local clubs and booze cans. Mixed in among them were a few gaunt insomniacs riding all night to escape the nightmares waiting for them at home. One woman had retreated into her own world, engaged in an animated discussion with her invisible friend. We all sat or stood against a backdrop of advertising posters that nagged us to eat, drink and spend our way to a holly jolly Christmas. If Hell exists, I'm sure one form of eternal damnation involves riding subway trains.

When I reached Laura's apartment building, the acne pocked kid was at the security desk. He must have been in a good mood because he gave me much less hassle than he had the last time. When the kid handed me the visitor's register to sign, I noticed that someone named Henry Fargo had signed in to visit Laura just a few minutes earlier. The name meant nothing to me, but I recognized the handwriting and felt the sour taste of fear in my mouth.

As I rode the elevator up to Laura's floor, I took my pistol out of my coat and pulled the cocking slide back. Keeping the gun at my side, I pushed the buzzer button at Laura's door. While I waited, I began to feel a little foolish. I was probably overreacting. Laura opened the door and moved back to let me come in. As I stepped through the doorway, I felt the cold metal of a gun muzzle pressed against the side of my head.

"Relax, Ryan," Beck said. "Let's have that gun of yours. Slow and easy."

Beck took my Glock and put his own pistol back into a pocket of his black overcoat. He walked to the center of the room, from where he could easily cover both Laura and me with my gun. Laura looked at me with a guilty expression on her face.

"I couldn't warn you, Matt. He said he'd kill us both if I did."

"It's all right, Laura."

"He told me his name was Detective Fargo and he had news about Eric's death."

"He's a cop all right, but his name is Joe Beck."

"You know him?" Laura asked.

"Ryan and I are old pals," Beck said. "Sit over there on the couch, Honey. I want to talk to your boyfriend for a minute."

Laura sat down on her black and white sofa.

"Why did you tell me your name was Fargo?" she asked.

"Let Ryan tell you. He has all the answers."

"Simple," I said. "Beck came here to kill you, so he wasn't going to sign in downstairs under his real name."

FORTY-THREE

Laura looked at Beck in amazement.

"You came here to kill me? Why? We've never even met before."

Beck shrugged.

"Let Ryan tell you. He's doing a great job of figuring things out."

"Beck killed Eric and Larry," I said. "He's tried to kill me at least twice. He was worried that you might know something about what happened at Shawncrest, so he was the one who broke into your apartment. He was looking for anything that might incriminate him."

"That about ties everything up," Beck said. "Nicely done."

Keeping his pistol aimed at me, Beck walked over to Laura's phone and pulled it out of its wall jack.

"That's better. I don't want us to be interrupted. It took you a long time to put the pieces together, Ryan. You're getting slow in your old age."

"You were very good, Beck, but you did make a few slips."

"Really? You've got me interested now. What slips?"

"When I told you I'd shot somebody at the garment factory, you said I was lucky to hit anything in the dark. I realized later I hadn't told you it was dark. You couldn't have known that without being there."

"Okay, that was careless. Anything else?"

"When I met you at Fran's, you kept your coat on inside a very warm restaurant. You didn't want me to see you had a bandage on your arm from where I'd shot you."

Beck winced as he flexed his left arm slightly.

"Still hurts like Hell sometimes," he said. "Your slug cut a groove across my tricep, just above the elbow. Is that everything?"

"Not quite. When David Raintree found Eric's body, he wrote the word 'hangman' in Eric's blood on the wall. It was his way of saying that Eric's death was punishment for what happened to Donald Prescott.

That gave you an idea. When you shot Larry, you wrote out that same word so people would think David had done it. You made one mistake. David had written the word in longhand, while you printed it in block letters. That made me think there were at least two people involved."

"Very clever. Any other slips?"

"No, but you were just a little too eager to convince me that Eric's death and Larry's weren't linked to Shawncrest Accademy."

"Terrific detective work," Beck said. "It's a shame it won't help you now."

Over Beck's shoulder, I saw Laura was still sitting on the couch. She'd picked up her burgundy silk purse from a nearby table and was clutching it against her body.

"Why did you kill Eric and Larry?" she asked Beck.

"They knew too much, Honey. I planned to whack Raintree too, but he was nice enough to take himself out and save me the trouble. Now, you and Ryan are the only loose ends left."

Beck grinned at me.

"This Glock of yours is nice, Ryan. I've got to get one of these babies."

Somehow, I had to keep Beck talking until I could think of a way out of this mess. The prospect of being shot to death with my own gun was sickening enough. What was even worse was the fact that Beck planned to kill Laura too. I realized suddenly how much I cared about her.

"We can settle this between us, Beck," I said. "Let Laura go."

"You must be kidding. If she didn't know too much before, she does now. I've just had a great idea, Ryan. You and your girlfriend were victims of a tragic murder suicide. First you shot her with this gun, then you killed yourself with it."

"Nobody will believe that."

"Why not? You're a recovered drunk who takes medication for depression. People won't find it hard to believe you flipped out. It'll be a very easy sell."

I knew he was right.

"What started all this?" I asked. "Jack Hornsby told me you couldn't solve the Prescott case, but I think you did."

"A six year old could've solved it, Ryan. When I checked that maintenance shed, there was still a short piece of rope tied around one of the rafters and an overturned chair on the floor. I found a rag stained with urine thrown into one corner. Prescott pissed himself when he was hung. It's a common reaction to strangulation. The perps wiped the mess off the floor, but left that rag lying around. I knew exactly what happened to the Prescott kid. All I had to do was to find his body and figure out who did it."

"Did you find the body?"

"Sure. Somebody mentioned an old well on the grounds and I figured that was probably where the kid's corpse had been dumped. I got a pry bar from the shed and pulled a couple of planks off the well cover. The stench coming out of that hole told me I was right."

"At least a couple of hundred boys were at Shawncrest," I said. "How did you know who was guilty?"

"That wasn't hard either. Several kids told me how Holt, Weisman and Raintree ran in a pack and tormented the younger boys. I brought each of them in individually for questioning. Holt and Weisman stuck to their alibis, but that weenie Raintree folded right away. He spilled the whole story."

"Why didn't you arrest them?"

"They were all minors. Even for a murder, the worst they faced was a few years years in Juvie. I had a better idea."

"You decided on blackmail," I said.

"Call it what you want. I got all the parents together and laid out what I knew before I hinted I might suffer amnesia if they made it worth my while. Nobody wanted a scandal. They jumped at the chance."

"How much did you get?"

"Fifty thousand from each family. That was coffee money to people like them. For a young cop, it was a lot of green. I wasn't stupid enough to run around spending it and drawing attention to myself. Instead, I put the cash into some conservative investments. They've done pretty well for me. I'll be able to retire ten years early and live some place where it's warm. No more crappy Toronto winters for me."

"It seems you thought of everything, Beck. What went wrong?"

"A couple of months ago, Raintree read about some landscaping scheduled at that faggot school. The faculty was going to open the old well again. Raintree knew they'd find Prescott's bones and he tried to talk the other two into coming forward with him to admit what they'd done. If they all confessed, everything would come out and I'd be nailed as an accessory to murder. I'd wind up doing more jail time than the three perps because they were minors when they killed Prescott. I wasn't going to let that happen."

"So you killed Eric and Larry," I said.

"I went to Weisman's shop just to reason with him, but Raintree had the guy spooked already. Weisman told me he'd had nightmares ever since the killing and it would be a relief to confess. I asked for a beer. When Weisman left the room to get one, I saw the shotgun he was cleaning. It was just a golden opportunity. I didn't know Raintree would show up later and write on the wall. When he did, it seemed like a great chance to pin the killing on him."

"What about Larry?"

"After I smoked Weisman, I knew Holt and Raintree had to go too. I called Holt and told him I had some questions about Weisman's death. He let me into his house and I blew his brains out. I wrote that word on the wall so it would look like Raintree killed Holt too."

"I knew you were a tough cop," I said. "I never thought of you as a killer."

Beck shrugged and sighed.

"You don't know how tired I am of all this, Ryan. It makes me a little sick. You're one of the few decent guys I've met, so I won't enjoy whacking you. I'll like killing your girlfriend here even less. No matter what, I'm not going to let myself go to prison. You know what happens to cops in prison."

I saw the look on Beck's face and knew I'd run out of time.

"Okay," he said. "Time for you to go bye bye, Ryan. If there's an afterlife, say hello to Raintree for me."

Beck raised the pistol to aim at my head. I flinched when I heard a shot, but realized I hadn't been hit. The Glock fell from Beck's hand as he sank to his knees. Behind him, Laura still sat on the couch, her open purse clutched in her left hand. In her right hand, she held the .38 Colt Cobra that I'd given to her.

Beck was on the floor now and blood trickled from the left side of his mouth as he looked up at me.

"I'm hit bad, Ryan. Call an ambulance. Please don't let me die."

Before I could pull out my cellphone, Laura got up from the couch and crossed the room to stand over Beck. She pointed her revolver down at him and I knew what she was going to do.

"Don't, Laura. He's not worth it."

"This is for Eric and Larry," Laura said.

She fired her gun at Beck until the hammer clicked on empty chambers. The big cop's body jerked from the impact of the bullets, but he was dead after the first one or two hit him. When Laura realized her Colt was empty, she let it fall to the floor and just stood there. I went over to her and she slumped against me sobbing.

"Oh, Matt! Was I wrong?"

"Yes. I might have done the same, but you were still wrong."

"This is so horrible. I'm a doctor. I took an oath to save lives, not kill. But when I thought about Eric and Larry..."

"I know," I said.

"Will I go to prison?"

"Not if I can help it. You saved my life. We can argue that the first bullet was self defense. The other five will be harder to explain."

"Should I call the police, Matt?"

"No. I have to think of a way to get us out of this."

Only one idea occurred to me and it was a remote chance at best. I took out my cellphone and was relieved to find I'd stored Yuri Kursov's number. After I made the call, I waited while Kursov's phone rang several times.

"Da?" said a gruff voice. It was my old pal Stone Face.

"This is Matt Ryan," I said. "I need to talk to Mr. Kursov right now. It's urgent."

Stone Face said something in Russian under his breath. I got the impression it was about me and wasn't a compliment.

"You wait," he said.

He put the phone down and I heard Kursov's voice a moment later.

"It is late, Mr. Ryan. Why are you calling me now?"

"You said once that you'd remember me if I needed help."

"What do you want?"

"I can't talk about it over the phone. May I come to your home?"

"When?" Kursov asked. He sounded slightly curious.

"In about half an hour?"

"Good. I will make coffee."

FORTY-FOUR

Laura had gone back to sit on her couch. She was trembling and kept her face turned away from Beck's dead body. I bent down to pick up my Glock and Laura's Colt from the floor before I put each of the guns into a separate pocket of my coat. After that, I walked over to stand in front of Laura.

"How are you doing, Kid?" I asked.

"Not good, Matt. I've never killed anybody before."

"You never get used to it. I have a plan. It's a risky one, but it's all we've got."

"What plan?"

"First, we need to get out of here and hope your neighbors didn't hear the shots. I don't have my car with me. Is yours downstairs?"

"Yes."

"Good. Get your keys. We need to leave right away."

Laura found her keys and got her coat. The two of us stepped out into the hallway. As Laura locked the door to her apartment, I looked up and down the corridor. I was relieved to see nobody around. Nobody else was in the elevator either while we rode down to the parking area. The garage still reeked of gasoline and tire rubber. We walked over to where Laura's Volvo was parked and I looked at Laura to see how well she was holding up.

"Feel up to driving?" I asked. "The roads are slippery tonight."

"I'll be fine, Matt. Driving will keep my mind off things."

We both got into her Volvo. Laura backed out of her parking spot, drove to the garage exit and we waited while the automatic door slowly went up. Finally, we went up the ramp to the street and I got a pleasant surprise for a change. The rain had stopped while I'd been inside and the air temperature had climbed two or three degrees. As a result, the slick sheet ice that coated the city pavements was quickly rotting into slush. Because of the lateness of the hour, city traffic was sparse and driving was more messy now than it was treacherous.

I'd been out to Kursov's house only once before and that was while I was tied up in the back of a van. I wasn't confident that I could find the place, especially at night. Fortunately, Laura's Volvo had one of those GPS navigation devices. While we waited at a traffic light, I gave Laura the name of Kursov's street and she keyed it into the system. After that, an eerie voice from the dashboard told us when to turn left or right. About twenty minutes later, I saw the Russian gangster's plantation style home ahead of us. We drove up to the large wrought iron gates and I had Laura tap the Volvo's horn twice.

"Yes?" squawked a voice from the intercom box that was fixed to one of the gate posts.

I rolled the window down on my side of the car.

"Matt Ryan," I said loudly. "Mr. Kursov is expecting me."

The gates swung open slowly, allowing us to drive up the long interlocking brick driveway and park in front of the house. I turned to look at Laura.

"These are very dangerous people," I said. "Maybe you'd better wait in the car."

"Sitting here all alone? Not a chance in Hell, Matt."

I realized I wasn't going to win this argument, so I shrugged.

"All right. Let's go."

We left Laura's Volvo and walked up the front steps of the house. I pressed the doorbell button and we waited. A couple of minutes later, Stone Face opened the door. He scowled at me before he looked at Laura with surprise. I could tell he'd expected me to be alone.

"You come in," he said in his gravel pit voice.

I expected Stone Face to grip my arm as he had on my previous visit, but he just turned and led us down the hallway. We walked into the same room where I'd first met Kursov. The gray haired mobster was there already, sitting in the same chocolate colored chair. On a table next to him, he had a silver coffee pot, some white china cups, a vodka bottle and six small glasses. Kursov stood up as Laura and I entered the room.

"Laura, meet Mr. Yuri Kursov," I said. "Kursov, this is Dr. Laura Weisman, Eric's sister."

Kursov took Laura's right hand and kissed the back of it.

"Enchanted, Dr. Weisman. My sorrow for the tragic death of your brother."

"Thank you," Laura said.

Kursov turned to Stone Face.

"Mikhail, bring another chair."

Stone Face fetched one small chair from a corner of the room and placed it near the others.

"*Spasibo*," Kursov said. "If we need anything else, I will call you."

Stone Face bowed and left the room.

"Please sit down," Kursov told us. "I have coffee or perhaps you would prefer vodka. It is Finnish, even better than Russian."

"Just coffee for me," I said as I sat down.

"I'll try a little of the vodka," Laura said.

Kursov filled one of the white china cups with coffee and handed it to me before he poured vodka into two of the small glasses. He gave one glass to Laura, then picked up the other one.

"*Nasdrovia*," he said, holding up his glass.

Laura sipped her vodka while Kursov tossed his drink down in a single gulp. When I tasted my coffee, it was strong enough to float an aircraft carrier and seemed to contain a kilogram of sugar. I put the cup back onto the table.

"That's a wonderful butterfly collection," Laura said as she pointed to the lighted display cases that had been arranged along one wall. Kursov grinned like a boy who'd just won a big football game for the team.

"You have an eye for beauty," he said. "Please examine them more closely while Mr. Ryan and I go into the next room and discuss some business."

FORTY-FIVE

For a moment, I thought Laura was going to give Kursov an argument and spoil everything, but she just nodded and walked over to look at the dead insects in their display cases. Kursov led me into a small adjoining room where a chessboard had been set up on an oblong marble topped table. Except for two chairs positioned at the chess table, the only other furniture in the room was a small mahogany writing desk. Kursov sat down at one end of the chess board and gestured for me to sit at the other end.

"Do you play chess, Mr. Ryan?"

"Yes, but not very well."

"We must have a game some day. I can tell much about a man by the way he plays chess."

"You may be right," I said.

"Tell me, Mr. Ryan. What is this favor that you need?"

"There's a dead man in Dr. Weisman's apartment. I want his body to disappear."

Kursov couldn't hide his surprise.

"May I ask how the man came to be dead?" he asked.

"He was shot in self defense, but it might be hard to prove. I should tell you that the dead man was a police officer."

Kursov steepled his fingers in front of him and looked at me. I could tell he wasn't enthusiastic about my request.

"A dead policeman, Mr. Ryan. This is a very large favor you ask of me."

I decided I'd been stupid to think Kursov would bail me out and I got up from my chair.

"Thanks for you time, Kursov. I apologize for calling on you so late at night. Laura and I can see ourselves out."

"Sit down," Kursov said.

I sensed this was an order, so I did as I was told.

"Have you had any visitors lately?" Kursov asked.

I looked at him blankly for a minute before the penny dropped.

"How did you know the Mounties have been around to see me?"

"There is little I do not know, Mr. Ryan. What did they want?"

"They wanted me to ask you for a job, so I could spy on you."

"And what did you tell them?"

"That I wasn't interested."

"That was very wise. I would have known at once that you were lying and it would have been very unpleasant for you. Did they tell you anything about me?"

I looked at Kursov and wondered how much of my soul I was prepared to sell.

"They have a mole inside your organization already," I said.

"And what is his name?"

"I don't know and I wouldn't tell you anyway. I don't want to sign somebody's death warrant."

Kursov nodded.

"You do not need to tell me. I know who it is. For some time, I have suspected him. Now, I am sure."

"Why would one of your people work for the Mounties?"

"Perhaps for money or maybe the police have charges against him that they will drop if he cooperates. It does not matter."

"What are you going to do?" I asked.

Kursov showed me a cruel smile.

"I will feed our little fish small pieces of information, but he will never learn anything important. When the time is right, he will pay for his treachery."

Kursov stood up and walked to the writing desk. He opened the top drawer of the desk, took out a pen and notepad, then put both items down on the chess table in front of me.

"You will give me three things," he said. "First, the address where the lovely Dr. Weisman lives. Second, the key to her apartment. Third, a phone number where you can be reached."

I scribbled Laura's address and my cellphone number onto the top page of the notepad before I handed the pad back to Kursov.

"Laura has her apartment key," I said, "but I'll get it for you before we leave."

"Good. Please take Dr. Weisman somewhere safe for tonight. Tomorrow, you will get a phone call. The caller will say only that your drycleaning is ready. When you hear this, you will know that everything has been taken care of."

"Thanks for doing this," I said.

"It is nothing. I know what you think of me, Mr. Ryan. Here in Canada, people believe that all Russians are crude and corrupt. They see Russia as a third world country with nuclear rockets. Sadly, they are right. Once, we were the nation of Tolstoy and Dostoyevsky. We had art and greatness. The Soviets brought Russia to her knees, then Yeltsin and the American capitalists cut her throat. When I look at what my country has become, I weep. I am the gangster you think I am, but I am also a man who pays his debts. My debt to you is now paid. Shall we go back and join Dr. Weisman?"

We walked back into the room where Kursov kept his butterfly collection. Laura had finished looking at it and she was back sitting in her chair as she sipped the last of her vodka. She looked up as we entered the room.

"Give Mr. Kursov your apartment keys," I said to Laura. "I'll explain later."

Laura handed her keys to Kursov before he called Stone Face to show us out. I was surprised when the Russian gangster shook hands with me and then he bowed to Laura.

"Good night, Mr. Ryan," Kursov said. "Dr. Weisman, I hope we will meet again, under happier circumstances."

"I look forward to it," Laura said. She flashed Kursov that smile of hers that melted most men into puddles at her feet.

Stone Face took Laura and me to the front door, then closed it behind us after we'd gone outside.

"What was that all about?" Laura asked as we walked down the front steps.

I told her about my conversation with Kursov. By now, we were at the car.

"This time, I'll drive," I said. "We can't risk having some cop stop you for a spot check and smelling vodka on your breath."

"People can't smell vodka on your breath, Matt."

"Just give me the keys. With our luck, we'll get stopped by a cop who's part bloodhound."

Laura made a face, but she handed me the ignition key. We got into the Volvo and I drove away from Kursov's home. Somehow, I found my way onto Highway 401 and headed east. Within a few minutes, we were back my place. After I parked the car, Laura turned around in the passenger's seat to look at me.

"Do you really think we can get away with this?" she asked.

"I hope so. If we get caught, we'll be in a lot more trouble than if we'd just called the cops back at your place. It'll be hard to convince a jury of our innocence after we've tried to hide Beck's body."

"The last two months have been a nightmare, Matt. I keep hoping I'll wake up to find that none of this really happened."

"If you do, please shake me awake too," I said.

"Can I stay here at your place tonight?"

"You don't need to ask. I'm sorry you've been through such a rough time, Laura. At least I get paid to risk my neck. You don't. Right now, we both need some sleep. Let's go inside."

We went up to my apartment. Laura had no personal stuff with her, so I told her she could use my toothbrush or whatever else she needed. Because we'd already slept together, it seemed silly for me to spend the night on the sofa. We both got undressed and climbed into my bed. As tired as we both were, neither of us even mentioned having sex. Within minutes after I turned off the bedside lamp, I was asleep.

Something was chasing me down a long corridor lit only by an eerie green glow. I didn't know what was back there, but I knew it would destroy me if it caught me. The corridor began sloping steeply upwards until I had trouble keeping my footing on the slippery floor.

Suddenly, I fell and slid back while I tried frantically to crawl forward. I heard laughter from above me and looked up. Eric Weisman leered down at me, his face half blown away by a shotgun blast. Next to him were Larry Holt and David Raintree, both bleeding from gaping wounds in their heads. All three were laughing and pointing behind me. I turned my head to look back and saw Joe Beck crawling toward me. He was spurting fountains of blood from the bullet holes in his body and he grinned insanely as he dragged the decayed corpse of Donny Prescott behind him on a rope.

Somebody was shaking me. I opened my eyes to find Laura looking at me with concern and I realized I must have been yelling in my sleep.

"Matt, what's wrong?"

"Sorry," I said. "Just a bad dream."

Laura draped left her arm over me and moved closer.

"You're safe now, Darling," she said. "Soon, it'll all be over."

I kissed her, then lay staring up at the ceiling after she'd fallen asleep again. The bad nights were back.

FORTY-SIX

Next morning, I was out of bed while Laura was still sleeping. I squinted at my wristwatch and saw that it was ten o'cock already. After showering, I inspected myself in the bathroom mirror while I shaved. The cut on my left cheek was just a red mark now and it might heal without leaving a scar. Bruises still marked my torso, but they were fading. If I could avoid being beaten or shot for the next few days, I might wind up being as good as new.

I pulled on a pale blue shirt and a pair of gray wool slacks before preparing breakfast. In honor of Laura's visit, I bypassed my usual whole grain cereal routine and tried scrambling some eggs. They came out much better than expected. I was toying with the idea of giving up detective work to become a chef when Laura came out of the bedroom.

"Morning," I said. "The bathroom's all yours. I'm fixing some breakfast. Sorry, but all I have is instant coffee."

"Instant will be fine, Matt. I'll be there in a minute."

Laura went into the bathroom and I heard the shower running. My cellphone rang as I was setting the dining table. I found the phone where I'd left it lying on a shelf.

"Hello?" I said.

"Your drycleaning is ready," said a voice with a heavy Russian accent. Before I could reply, the caller hung up.

I was sipping pink grapefruit juice when Laura came out of the bathroom. She looked gorgeous. I've never understood how women transform themselves, but it's obviously a form of magic we mere men will never master.

"I just got the call we were expecting," I said. "We can go back to your apartment later."

Laura sat down at the table and looked at me.

"I can't go back there, Matt. I just can't. Every time I look at the floor, I'll see that man's body. As it is, I'll be haunted for the rest of my life by what I've done."

"I understand, Laura. I just meant we can go back so you can pack some clothes and personal effects. Do you own that condo or do you lease it?"

"I bought it, but there's still a mortgage."

"Fine. Have the place cleaned up and then sell it. The new owners don't need to know what happened there."

"Where will I live in the meantime?"

"You can stay here until you can find a new place."

"That's sweet of you, Matt, but I've imposed on you too much already. I can find a hotel. It would be different if you felt the same way about me that I do about you."

We were back to that again. I reached out and touched Laura's arm.

"Look, Laura. We've been through a lot together. I'm not even sure we're out of the woods yet. Whatever happens, I owe you my life. I wouldn't say you could stay here if I didn't mean it. Anyway, it's just for a little while. Just until you can find somewhere."

"All right. Thanks."

"I hope you like scrambled eggs. I can make toast too, if you like."

"Just eggs and coffee will be fine, Matt. I'm still having some drug withdrawal symptoms and my appetite is down."

Two hours later, we were in Laura's Volvo and stopped in front of her apartment building. Laura used her garage access card to get into the parking area. From there, we took the elevator to her floor without having to sign in at the reception desk. That was fine with me. I didn't want to field any questions from Jack Hornsby.

When we opened the door to Laura's apartment, the place smelled of carpet shampoo. Kursov's team had done a first rate job. Beck's body was gone and the whole place had been cleaned meticulously. A forensics team might have found specks of blood or human DNA, but no casual observer would have guessed that anything unusual had happened in the place.

Laura seemed nervous, anxious to collect her belongings and get out as soon as possible. While she hurried with her packing, I stood at one of the apartment's windows and watched traffic move through the city streets, nineteen floors below. I thought about how urban life is a toxic drug that gets into your bloodstream, leaving you strung out and burned out. You curse the loneliness and swear to yourself that you'll go somewhere else, anywhere else. Another day dawns and you're still here, hooked on the noise and the glitz, seduced by the lie that tomorrow will be better.

Finally, Laura was ready. She'd packed two suitcases and an overnight bag with enough cosmetics and clothing to sustain her for a while. We locked the apartment again before I helped Laura carry her luggage down to her car. A few minutes later, we were driving back to my place.

"I really need to go into my office today," Laura said. "I've been away from my patients too long already. My nurse Stanley is a real trouper and he's handled things beautifully, but he can't hold the fort forever."

"Drop me and your luggage at my apartment," I said. "You'd be better off to leave your car there too. Take the TTC downtown. You'll get there faster and with no parking hassles."

Laura followed my advice. After she was gone, I stowed her bags in one corner of my bedroom, ready for her to unpack later. Before I could take off my parka and relax, I had one more thing to do. I opened the desk drawer where I'd stowed Laura's .38 Cobra, took the revolver out and shoved it into my right hand pocket.

After I collected my Toyota from the parking lot, I drove southward on the Don Valley Parkway before I took Bay Street down to Queen's Quay and the ferry docks. Standing on the docks, I looked around me. It was a gloomy day and a bitter wind whipped in off the water. The Center Island ferry had sailed a few minutes earlier, leaving the docking slip deserted and very few people were walking by on the street. When nobody was in sight, I pulled the .38 Cobra out of my coat and threw it as far out into Lake Ontario as I could. After that, I drove home.

Back in my apartment, I was heating water to brew some tea when the white plastic intercom panel buzzed on the kitchen wall. Somebody was calling from the lobby. I walked over and pressed the talk button.

"Yes?" I asked.

"Glad I caught you home, Ryan. Can I come up? I've got something to tell you."

"Go away, Flynn. I'm tired of your games. I'm not going to do your dirty work, so either arrest me or get out of my life."

"Call me Jimmy. Lose the attitude, Ryan. I think you'll like what I have to say. Do I get to come up or what?"

With a sigh, I switched off the electric kettle.

"Take the elevator to the fourth floor, Flynn. Turn right in the hallway. It's Apartment 412."

Two minutes later, I heard Flynn's knock at my door.

FORTY-SEVEN

Flynn was bundled up in a tan trench coat and wore a burgundy wool scarf. His cheeks were flushed and his eyes seemed a little too bright. I suspected he'd been drinking some Christmas cheer. As he stood in the hallway, he gave me one of his tobacco stained smiles.

"Don't I get to come in?" he asked.

"Where are my manners?" I said.

I stepped back as Flynn walked in. I was trying not to show how nervous he made me feel. If Flynn knew anything about Beck's death, I was finished. Flynn looked around at my apartment before he nodded.

"Not bad, Ryan. I expected something shabbier."

"I'm sure this isn't your first time here, Flynn. Or did you send somebody else to search the place and plant the bugs."

Flynn shrugged his way out of his coat and scarf before he tossed them both onto my couch. Without being asked, he pulled up a chair and sat down.

"I've no idea what you're talking about, Ryan. Got anything to drink?"

"Just fruit juice. I don't think that's what you meant."

"Hell, no. You're not much of a host, Ryan."

"Not when people invite themselves. Why are you here?"

"Call me, Jimmy. I just wanted to deliver some good news. You're license has been reinstated. Tomorrow, some of our people will be at your office to return all your records."

"That is good news. Why the change of heart?"

"I feel like playing Santa Claus. Also, we don't need you any more, Ryan. Remember how my chatty partner told you we had a mole inside Kursov's organization?"

"I remember."

"Well, our snitch gave us a copy of a DVD that contains some files that are very incriminating to Kursov. The mole told us that Kursov got the disk from some private dick. Any idea who that could be?"

"Not a clue," I said.

"Didn't think so. Anyway, the data on the DVD isn't enough to bring Kursov down by itself, but it'll justify a search of his house and audits of his business fronts. We'll troll through his bank accounts, company books and tax forms. Hell, we'll comb through his underwear drawer. If Kursov's hiding so much as an unpaid speeding ticket, we'll find it. The guy is toast."

"You must really want Kursov pretty badly."

"We don't give a shit about Kursov. It's his bosses back in Moscow we're after. When Kursov faces a few hundred years in the slammer, he'll cut a deal to give us the guys above him on the food chain."

"Use the small fish to catch the bigger fish. Is that it?" I asked.

"That's always been the game, Ryan. You should know that."

"Your mole must be due for a big reward."

"He'll probably never collect," Flynn said.

"What do you mean?"

"Nobody's seen him for a couple of days. Maybe he just took a trip, but I think his cover got blown. If that's true, he's dead. I've heard how the Russians punish informers. When they finally got around to slitting his throat, the guy was probably grateful."

"Who was he?" I asked.

"A mean little knife toting weasel named Sascha Gorshenko. I doubt you've ever met the bastard."

"Your right. The name doesn't ring a bell."

"Well, that's about it, Ryan. You're in the clear now. Nothing personal about how I was squeezing you. Just doing my job."

"If I had a job like yours, I'd find another one," I said.

Flynn shrugged.

"Easy for you to say, Pal. Tell that to my wife in the suburbs and my two daughters in private schools."

A little unsteadily, he stood up and retrieved his coat and scarf before he started toward the door. I was surprised when he stopped, turned around and held out his hand.

"Merry Christmas, Ryan. From one mick to another."

I considered telling him to go to Hell, but shook his hand instead.

"*Nollaig Shona Duit,*" I said. "Merry Christmas."

"You speak Irish?"

"You've just heard my entire vocabulary."

Flynn laughed and winked at me.

"You're a cute one, Ryan. Keep your nose clean. I'd hate to have to bust you for real. By the way, we did search your place, but we didn't plant any bugs. You and that hot Jewish girlfriend of yours will have complete privacy. You lucky bastard."

With that, he left my apartment. I walked over from the doorway and sat down on my sofa. Was everything finally over? I knew I should feel relieved, but I didn't. How much had what I'd told Kursov about an informer contributed to Sascha's death? Certainly, the man had been a nasty piece of work, but that didn't make things right. Laura had one death on her conscience. Now, I might have two.

FORTY-EIGHT

Rosedale looked as rich and exclusive as ever when I parked my car in the driveway at the Raintree house. I pulled a black computer bag out of the trunk before I walked up the steps and rang the doorbell. When Rebecca Raintree opened the door, she was wearing a black dress and no makeup. Her eyes were red. I knew she'd deny it, but I suspected she'd been crying.

"Hello, Mr. Ryan," she said. "I was surprised when you called."

"I wanted to return David's computer and to tell you how sorry I am."

"Thank you. I've been told you were with David when he..."

"Yes, Ma'am. I was there."

"I don't understand. Why would David kill himself?"

I decided Mrs. Raintree didn't need to know about Shawncrest.

"He was very depressed, " I said. "It's a brain disorder that I suffer from myself, but I take medication that helps me function. It's still hard for me to focus sometimes. For David, I guess the medication wasn't enough."

"I can't believe he's gone," Mrs. Raintree said. She seemed to be on the verge of tears again.

"The Irish say that a man's not really dead so long as there's one person alive who remembers him, Mrs. Raintree. You're still here to remember David."

"Not for long. I'm an old woman."

"He'll still have more immortality than most of us."

"Thank you, Mr. Ryan,. I know you're only trying to help. Do I owe you anything more for your investigation?"

"No, Ma'am."

"Well, goodbye then."

She took the computer from me and closed the door. I walked back to my car, leaving her alone in that empty house with only grief for companionship. As I drove home, I felt like a soldier who'd survived a war but had no idea what to do with the peace. When I was back in my apartment, I picked up the telephone and called Samantha. She answered after three rings.

"Matt, I haven't heard from you in days," she said.

"A lot has happened. I'll fill you in on the details later. It's over, Sam. The man who tried to kill me is dead and the Mounties are off my back. We can get on with our lives."

"Matt, I have something to tell you."

"Go ahead."

"Day before yesterday, I got a phone call from Sherry Walker. She's an old friend of mine. We went to highschool together and were like sisters. She was in Toronto for a couple of days to attend a business conference."

"That's great, Sam."

"Five years ago, Sherry moved out to Alberta with her husband. They divorced later and she started an advertising agency in Calgary to support herself. She's been very successful at it."

"Wonderful. Can I come over tonight?"

"She offered me a job with her agency, Matt. I accepted."

I sat there for a moment while Sam's words sank in.

"A job?" I said stupidly. "In Calgary?"

"Matt, I didn't want to tell you this way, but I'm such a coward. It's easier to do this over the phone instead of face to face."

"When are you going?" I asked. I seemed to hear my own voice from far away.

"Sherry wants me to start by next week. Tess and I will be leaving day after tomorrow. I can fly back to Toronto later to finish packing my things and my lawyer will handle sale of the house. Sherry's going to arrange for a private tutor for Tess, so she won't miss her school year. I'm so sorry, Matt."

"Why are you doing this, Sam?"

197

"I thought I could handle things, Matt. Worrying myself to death every time you go out on a case. Never knowing when I'll get a phone call telling me you've been killed. When that awful man shot at you and Tess, I knew I couldn't do it anymore. I love you, but I won't put Tess in danger."

"I told you that guy is dead, Sam. I've finished the Raintree case."

"Don't you see, Matt? There will always be other cases."

She was right.

"So, is that it then?" I asked. "We're finished?"

"I'm so sorry, Darling. Tess wants to speak to you."

"Hello, Matt," Theresa said.

"Hi, Tess." I said in a daze.

"Mommy says we have to go away."

"I know, Honey."

"I don't want to go.

"Sometimes we have to do things we don't want to do, Tess."

"Does this mean I'll never see you again?"

"Of course not, Honey. I can come out for visits. You can write to me or send emails..."

My voice trailed off because we both knew it wouldn't happen that way.

"I'll miss you you, Matt."

"I'll miss you too, Tess."

"Here's Mommy again."

"Matt, It'll be better if I don't see you again before we leave. If I do, I'm afraid I'll change my mind. Goodbye, Darling."

Samantha hung up her phone and I sat there, staring at the wall. I still looked the same, but my insides had just been kicked out.

FORTY-NINE

When Laura came home from work, I was sitting near the dining room window as I watched snow fall outside. Nature was providing a soft white blanket for a city of broken dreams. Laura took off her boots and hung up her coat before she came over to kiss my cheek. She was carrying a newspaper.

"Hello, Darling," she said. "I hope this snow won't amount to much. I'm always terrified about driving on slippery roads. How was your day?"

"I've had better ones."

"What's wrong, Matt. You look really down. Did something happen? Was it to do with... you know... ?"

She held out the day's edition of *The Toronto Star*. On the front page was a photo of Beck and the headline "Police Officer Missing".

"Nothing like that," I said. "As a matter of fact, one of the Mounties came by to tell me they're going to reinstate my license and stop harrassing me."

"That's wonderful! You should be sipping champagne, not looking glum. Have you told Samantha yet? See? I can remember her name when I put my mind to it."

"Samantha's moving out to Alberta. She dumped me."

"I'm so sorry, Matt. I mean that. What happened?"

"Samantha is just like Jane. Neither of them wants a guy who might come home from work in a pine box. Samantha has to think of her daughter too, so I guess I can't blame her."

"Those women didn't know how lucky they were," Laura said. "I wouldn't make the same mistake, if I could get you to love me."

I looked up at Laura and saw the longing on her face.

"Any guy would have to be an idiot not to fall in love with you, Laura. Maybe I'm an idiot too, but I've already fallen for two women who couldn't bear what I do for a living. I'm in no hurry to go through that emotional meat grinder again."

"It wouldn't be like that with us, Matt. I don't see how we could experience much worse than what we've been through already. Besides, the fact that you're life is a little dangerous excites me. You know that."

"Give me some time, Laura."

"As much time as you need, Darling. I won't give up on you easily. You're worth waiting for."

"Thanks. Let's talk about something else."

"All right. Who will you get to replace Samantha at the office?"

"I haven't even thought about that yet."

"What about hiring me?"

"Be serious, Laura."

"What makes you think I'm not?"

"You're a doctor."

"Only because that was what my father wanted. I've been doing a lot of thinking about my life lately. It's time I found out what I want."

"I need an experienced assistant investigator, Laura. The job isn't as simple as you might think. It took me more than six months to train Samantha."

"I won't take that long, Darling. I'm a very quick study."

"Aside from filing and keeping the books, you'd spend most of your time running traces on people. You'd be bored to tears."

"Didn't you ever let Samantha do any field work, Matt?"

"Sometimes, when it wasn't too dangerous."

"Then I could do that too. I realize now what a mess my life was before I met you. That's why I started doing drugs. I think working with you would be great. At least consider the idea."

"I couldn't pay you more than chicken feed anyway."

"When Daddy died, he left me some money. I'll work for free until I'm fully trained."

"You're making my head spin, Laura. I can't deal with all this right now. Let's talk about something else."

"All right. Christmas will be here in a couple of days. Are you looking forward to it?"

"I try to ignore Christmas. It has no religious significance for me any more. The idea of families and friends getting together is fine, but I hate all the commercialism and phoney sentimentality."

"My family wasn't religious either, but Mother had a menorah and we'd always light candles during Hanukka. It was nice. When Mother died, I'd observe the Hanukka rituals in her memory. Because of Eric's death and Larry's, I've missed Hanukka completely this year."

"I'm sorry about that, Laura."

"Don't be. I'm a Jew, so Christmas has no religious meaning for me either. Still, I've always liked it as a holiday. This is no time of year to be alone, Matt. Let's celebrate Christmas together."

"I prefer New Year's Eve," I said.

"Why is that?"

"Because I always have the crazy notion that the new year will be better than the old one. Why don't we spend both Christmas and New Year's Eve with each other and see how it goes?"

Laura sat on my lap and threw her arms around my neck.

"You really are a smooth talker, Darling," she said.

The End